Opening up
2 Chronicles

ANDREW THOMSON

DayOne

Opening up
2 Chronicles
ANDREW THOMSON

If you are reading 2 Chronicles and Andrew Thomson's exposition as you do so, you will say, 'My, how immensely practical 2 Chronicles is—I must dig into it even more!' And at that point you will, I suspect, have fallen into Mr Thomson's trap. He 'opens up' 2 Chronicles so that you will 'fall in'!

Dale Ralph Davis, former Professor of Old Testament, Reformed Theological Seminary, Jackson, MS, and former Pastor, Woodland Presbyterian Church, Hattiesburg, MS, USA

What Andrew Thomson did for the twenty-nine chapters of 1 Chronicles he has done again for the thirty-six chapters of 2 Chronicles. He has skilfully picked out the important teaching of 2 Chronicles and shown how God's care of his people continues, despite their unfaithfulness. Very easy to read, the book is crammed full of Scripture and includes many helpful, up-to-date illustrations.

Michael Bentley, retired evangelical pastor, Bracknell, UK

© Day One Publications 2011

First printed 2011

Unless otherwise indicated, all Scripture quotations are from the English Standard Version, Collins, 2002.

All rights reserved.

ISBN 978-1-84625-290-7

British Library Cataloguing in Publication Data available

Published by Day One Publications

Ryelands Road, Leominster, England, HR6 8NZ

Telephone 01568 613 740   FAX 01568 611 473

email—sales@dayone.co.uk

web site—www.dayone.co.uk

North American e-mail—usasales@dayone.co.uk

North American web site—www.dayonebookstore.com

Printed by Thomson Litho, East Kilbride

Dedication

In gratitude to the God who has transferred me to the kingdom of his beloved Son, which endures from generation to generation, with thanks for those of the generation before me who have been such an encouragement, especially Peter Seccombe, Bill Summers and Malcolm Evans, and with prayer for the next generation, especially Esther, Gemma, Joel, Laura, Roger, Kathryn, Sarah, James, Stephen, Thomas, Joanna, Natalie, Hannah and Rachel—that they (like Josiah) will seek the Lord while they are young.

930 BC

Rehoboam, who didn't set his heart to seek the Lord

Abijah, who preached to his enemy

Asa, the good king who ended badly

Jehoshaphat, the good king with bad allies

Jehoram, whom no one missed

Ahaziah, the bad king with a good grandfather

Joash, the bad king with a good priest

These blocks are drawn to scale to represent the length of each king's reign.

Amaziah, who turned away

Uzziah, the good king who became proud

Jotham, who ordered his ways

Ahaz, who was very unfaithful

Hezekiah, who was faithful

The shaded blocks represent the reigns of the kings who receive the highest praise in 2 Chronicles.

Manasseh, who repented

Amon, who didn't humble himself

Josiah, who had a tender heart

Jehoahaz

Jehoiakim

Jechoiachin

586 BC **Zedekiah**

OPENING UP 2 CHRONICLES

Contents

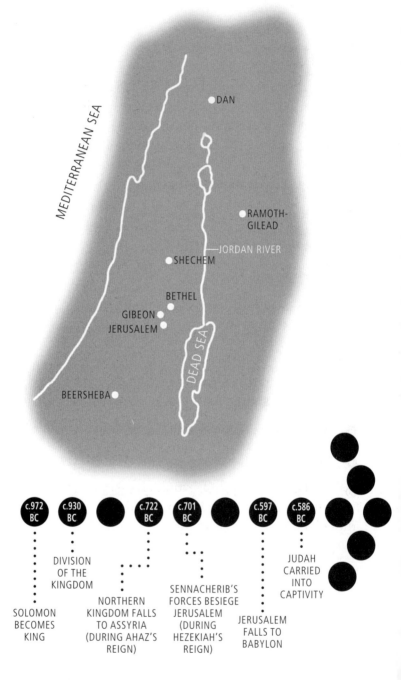

MEDITERRANEAN SEA

●DAN

●RAMOTH-
GILEAD

─JORDAN RIVER

●SHECHEM

BETHEL
●

GIBEON ●
JERUSALEM ●

DEAD SEA

BEERSHEBA●

| c.972 BC | c.930 BC | | c.722 BC | c.701 BC | | c.597 BC | c.586 BC |

DIVISION
OF THE
KINGDOM

NORTHERN
KINGDOM FALLS
TO ASSYRIA
(DURING AHAZ'S
REIGN)

SENNACHERIB'S
FORCES BESIEGE
JERUSALEM
(DURING
HEZEKIAH'S
REIGN)

JUDAH
CARRIED
INTO
CAPTIVITY

SOLOMON
BECOMES
KING

JERUSALEM
FALLS TO
BABYLON

OPENING UP 2 CHRONICLES

Overview

David has gone. The kingdom hasn't. Now we're invited on a roller-coaster ride tracing the ups and downs of this kingdom and its people for over four centuries. The first book of Chronicles undoubtedly focused on David, but there is life after David. In fact, David's reign is largely seen as one of preparation for Solomon's. Finally, the temple is to be built as a peaceful kingdom flourishes. But no sooner has Solomon 'excelled all the kings of the earth in riches and in wisdom' (9:22) than he is handing over the kingdom to a singularly unwise son. The kingdom of Israel splits in two, and Solomon's son is left with only a sixth of the kingdom to hand on to his successor. The next 350 years chart a decline in what is now the kingdom of Judah. The line on the graph shows a few promising upturns under the reign of a handful of kings, but it all too quickly resumes its downward course. Before we know it, Judah is swallowed up by the kingdom of Babylon, which in turn falls to the kingdom of Persia. But even these kingdoms are fulfilling the Word of the Lord. His warnings were no idle threats, but, equally, his promises won't fail. Israel is down but not out. The Lord will remember his covenant—even though his people often don't.

List of Bible abbreviations

THE OLD TESTAMENT					
		1 Chr.	1 Chronicles	Dan.	Daniel
		2 Chr.	2 Chronicles	Hosea	Hosea
Gen.	Genesis	Ezra	Ezra	Joel	Joel
Exod.	Exodus	Neh.	Nehemiah	Amos	Amos
Lev.	Leviticus	Esth.	Esther	Obad.	Obadiah
Num.	Numbers	Job	Job	Jonah	Jonah
Deut.	Deuteronomy	Ps.	Psalms	Micah	Micah
Josh.	Joshua	Prov.	Proverbs	Nahum	Nahum
Judg.	Judges	Eccles.	Ecclesiastes	Hab.	Habakkuk
Ruth	Ruth	S.of S.	Song of Solomon	Zeph.	Zephaniah
1 Sam.	1 Samuel	Isa.	Isaiah	Hag.	Haggai
2 Sam.	2 Samuel	Jer.	Jeremiah	Zech.	Zechariah
1 Kings	1 Kings	Lam.	Lamentations	Mal.	Malachi
2 Kings	2 Kings	Ezek.	Ezekiel		

THE NEW TESTAMENT					
		Gal.	Galatians	Heb.	Hebrews
		Eph.	Ephesians	James	James
Matt.	Matthew	Phil.	Philippians	1 Peter	1 Peter
Mark	Mark	Col.	Colossians	2 Peter	2 Peter
Luke	Luke	1 Thes.	1 Thessalonians	1 John	1 John
John	John	2 Thes.	2 Thessalonians	2 John	2 John
Acts	Acts	1 Tim.	1 Timothy	3 John	3 John
Rom.	Romans	2 Tim.	2 Timothy	Jude	Jude
1 Cor.	1 Corinthians	Titus	Titus	Rev.	Revelation
2 Cor.	2 Corinthians	Philem.	Philemon		

An outline of 1 & 2 Chronicles

Endless genealogies! (1 Chr. 1–9)

Endless kingdom! (1 Chr. 10–2 Chr. 36)

The kingdom of David

–Preparing for the temple (1 Chr. 11–29)

The kingdom of Solomon

–Building the temple (2 Chr. 1–9)

The kingdom of Judah

–Neglecting or valuing the temple (2 Chr. 10–35)

The kingdoms of Babylon & Persia

–Burning and rebuilding the temple (2 Chr. 36)

Part 1
The kingdom of Solomon

1 Worship, wisdom and wealth

(1:1–17)

David's kingdom appears to be in safe hands as 2 Chronicles begins. Worship is a good place to start for any kingdom. Next, we learn where Solomon's priorities lie, and happily they lie in the right place. We are told that Solomon establishes himself, but it is made clear that he only succeeds because, in reality, the Lord is establishing him. What is encouraging is that Solomon knows it, and knows that the right response is worship.

Worship (vv. 1–6)

The kingdom is at a high point, and Solomon gathers the people together at 'the great high place' (1 Kings 3:4) at Gibeon. Why Gibeon? The tent of meeting, and especially the altar, is there. Solomon is making two statements. The first is 'This marks a new beginning'.

The new beginning to end all new beginnings had taken place in the days of Noah. And that began with the building of an altar, and with burnt offerings too (Gen. 8:20). Abram's new beginning in the land of Canaan had also been marked by altar-building (Gen. 12:7). Hundreds of years later, when Joshua finally led the people into the promised land, we find the same symbolic act repeated.

But here in Solomon's time it isn't just about a new beginning. These offerings are also saying, 'Here is an expression of renewed commitment.' This is a kind of re-enactment of the scene on Mount Ebal, when Joshua had also built an altar and offered burnt offerings (Josh. 8:30–31). That was not just a fresh start, but also a symbolic renewing of the covenant, as the formal reading of 'the Book of the Law' at that time indicated (Josh. 8:34).

There is symbolism in the burnt offering, too. This was an offering primarily expressing dedication to God and seeking his acceptance (Lev. 1:3). '[A]ll of it' (Lev. 1:9, 13) was burnt on the altar, in contrast to the other offerings described in the book of Leviticus. When the apostle Paul urged the Christians at Rome to '... present your bodies as a living sacrifice, holy and acceptable to God' (Rom. 12:1), he was telling them to do what the burnt offering merely pictured. But the problem with a living sacrifice, as someone once observed, is that it keeps crawling off the altar. So we will have to be regularly dragging ourselves back to a place where we can sincerely

> The problem with a living sacrifice, as someone once observed, is that it keeps crawling off the altar.

sing, 'I surrender all'.[1] It may help to remind ourselves of the words of another hymn-writer: that 'we never can prove the delights of His love until all on the altar we lay'.[2]

But how can what we have to offer ever be enough? Solomon seems to have felt this problem. Why choose a thousand burnt offerings (2 Chr. 1:6)? Why stop there? Wouldn't two thousand be doubly acceptable to the Lord? As Micah would later ask, 'Will the LORD be pleased with thousands of rams, with ten thousands of rivers of oil?' (Micah 6:7). Every animal offered had to be without blemish (Lev. 1:3, 10), but the problem was that the same could not be said of the one for whom it was offered. None of us can claim to be blame-free and spotless. Some of us, though, can claim to have a Saviour who 'offered himself without blemish to God' (Heb. 9:14)—and his sacrifice is worth more than ten thousand burnt offerings.

Wisdom (vv. 7–13)

If you were given just one wish that would certainly be granted, what you asked for would say a lot about you. The story is told of the British ambassador to the United States being contacted by a TV reporter in Washington. The reporter wanted to know what the ambassador would like for Christmas. Reluctant to answer at first, the ambassador, when pressed, finally admitted that he would like a jar of mint jelly. Some weeks later, long after the conversation had been forgotten, he found himself watching TV when a programme entitled *The Spirit of Christmas* came on. A number of dignitaries had been interviewed about their wishes for the Christmas season. As the piece proceeded, the ambassador became more and more uncomfortable. The German ambassador wished for a peaceful and prosperous year ahead for all citizens of the planet. The Swiss ambassador desired that the world's leaders would be guided towards a common goal of peaceful co-existence. By now the British ambassador was squirming, waiting for the inevitable: '… and the British ambassador told us that he would like a jar of mint jelly.' What you ask for, what you really want, says a lot about you. If we are asked about our priorities, we may know enough to give the 'right' answer, but our lives may well tell a different story. We may read the Greek myth of King Midas, who asked that everything he touched might turn to gold, and we may laugh at his stupidity—but I fear that 'winning the lottery' would be the honest wish of a frightening number of people today. Most Christians would stop short of admitting any interest in gambling, but 'an easy life' often seems to be our number one priority.

Happily, when God asks him what he wants, Solomon is wise enough to ask for wisdom (vv. 7–10)! His request is coupled with a real confidence in the Lord that has its roots in his grasp of God's faithfulness towards his father (v. 8). James surely had this episode in mind when he wrote, 'If any of you lacks wisdom, let him ask God, who gives generously to all without reproach, and it will be given him. But let him ask in faith, with no doubting' (James 1:5–6).

Not only does Solomon have a healthy appreciation of the faithfulness of God, he has an equally important grasp of his own limitations. While Moses' 'Who am I?' response to God's command (Exod. 3:11) led to excuses, followed by the request to 'send someone else' (Exod. 4:13), Solomon's sense of inadequacy leads to prayer. Whenever we feel that something the Lord has given us to do is beyond us, it's good to look to God and remind ourselves that nothing is beyond him. That's what Paul does when he writes to the Corinthians. As he thinks of the solemn responsibility of preaching the gospel he asks, 'Who is sufficient for these things?' (2 Cor. 2:16), supplying the answer in the next chapter: 'our sufficiency is from God' (2 Cor. 3:5). That is always the answer. Of course, we need to be sure that the task we are about to tackle is the Lord's will for us, but if we have that assurance we can know that he will equip us for the work to which he calls us.

Solomon's priority is clearly the kingdom, and our Lord has assured us that if we seek the kingdom first, the less important things 'will be added to [us]' (Matt. 6:33). So it is here. The Lord knows that Solomon's request has come from his heart rather than from any sense of spiritual correctness. As a result, he promises to add 'riches, possessions, and honour' to the wisdom and knowledge the king has asked for (v. 12). No one could accuse Solomon of asking 'wrongly, to spend it on [his] passions'—the kind of selfish praying that James warns us about (James 4:3). Instead, we have been taught to pray, 'Your kingdom come' (Matt. 6:10), and if that prayer comes from the heart, God's kingdom will be our number one priority, just as it was Solomon's.

Wealth (vv. 14–17)

Back in 1 Chronicles, we saw how the writer was interested in David and Solomon in their official capacity as king. Their personal lives were not his concern. The glory of the kingdom is what he wanted to get across. So in 1 and 2 Chronicles we never hear about Solomon's old age, when his heart is 'turned away' from the Lord (1 Kings 11:4). It isn't a matter of a whitewash—the account we have in 1 Kings would have been well known. But the paragraph at the end of 2 Chronicles 1 contains enough information for the astute reader to pick up a kind of sub-text. And in case we miss it, the author repeats the same facts at the close of Solomon's reign in chapter 9 (vv. 27–28). We are told how common 'the king made silver and gold' (1:15) in Jerusalem, and about his 12,000 horsemen and his 'import of horses ... from Egypt' (v. 16). So what?

Well, we have been encouraged by Solomon's wise start in his official capacity as king, but where should he have started on a personal level? Surely where Joshua had started—with the Book of the Law (Josh. 1:8). And there was a special section there (in Deut. 17) just for Solomon. What did it have to say to the king? 'Only he must not acquire many horses for himself or cause the people to return to Egypt in order to acquire many horses ... nor shall he acquire for himself excessive silver and gold' (Deut. 17:16–17). All might be well in terms of the kingdom, but it looks as if the writer is subtly giving us a heads-up that the seeds of Solomon's tragic decline are already being sown. His mistake is all too reminiscent of that of Israel's first king, Saul. If only someone had asked Solomon what Samuel had asked Saul: 'Has the LORD as great delight in burnt offerings and sacrifices, as in obeying the voice of the LORD?' (1 Sam. 15:22). The answer to that question is 'No'. A thousand sacrifices are no substitute for careful obedience (1 Chr. 22:13).

FOR FURTHER STUDY

1. Read Hebrews 13:15–16 and 1 Peter 2:5. What offerings is it appropriate for the Christian to offer?

2. Read James 1:2–5 and 3:13–18. What do *we* need wisdom for, and what characteristics of 'the wisdom … from above' are most surprising and generally overlooked?

3. Read Matthew 6:19–34. What clues are there in this passage as to what seeking the kingdom of God first will actually look like in everyday life?

TO THINK ABOUT AND DISCUSS

1. Do you currently feel the need of a new beginning? What would a renewed commitment to the Lord involve for you?

2. Which areas of your life leave you feeling most aware of your need for wisdom?

3. What do you really want at the moment, and how sure are you that it is the Lord's will for you to have it?

4. Which matters of simple obedience tend to get overlooked in the church today? Have you ever failed to spot a personal area of disobedience for quite a while?

2 Great house, greater God

(2:1–6:42)

The temple is now to be built. The house will have its limitations (just like Solomon himself), but it will reflect, and ultimately be filled with, the glory of God.

The house that Solomon built (2:1–5:1)

'Whatever your hand finds to do, do it with your might' (Eccles. 9:10). That is certainly Solomon's approach. There is no self-confidence, but there is a determination to 'do all to the glory of God' (1 Cor. 10:31). He is aware of the magnitude of the task ahead of him. He is to build a house 'for the name of the LORD' (2:4)—to represent his character and special presence—so it needs to be 'great and wonderful' (2:9). This will require only the best materials and workmen, so Solomon prepares carefully, enlisting the help of the king of Tyre. As he does so, Solomon takes the opportunity to speak of the greatness of his God (2:5). There were many times in Israel's history when the nations around them would exercise a harmful influence on them, but here we see the kingdom at its best, exercising a good influence on neighbouring countries.

The same is to be true of the Christian church. All too often, the world influences the church, but there are times when the church fulfils its purpose and is salt and light in a decaying, dark world. Here Solomon is letting his 'light shine before others, so that they [might] see [his] good works and give glory' to his God (Matt. 5:16). That is precisely what Hiram goes on to do. He recognizes that Solomon is God's gift to Israel (2:12), to ensure that the temple is built. His language reminds us of another demonstration of God's love: the gift of someone not just to Israel, but to the whole world, 'that whoever believes in him should not perish but have eternal life' (John 3:16).

Hiram's wholehearted response and the involvement of Huram-abi (2:13) are a reminder to us—just as the Lord Jesus had to remind the people of his day—that this building was to be 'a house ... for all the nations' (Mark 11:17). With the promise of wood, the loan of a skilled craftsman and a workforce in place, the work is ready to begin. Solomon has already pointed out that the temple is 'a place to make offerings' (2:6), and before the work begins the writer reminds us that the location has associations with two earlier, momentous sacrifices (3:1). This was where Isaac was spared Abraham's knife in the nick of time (Gen. 22:10–13), and where Jerusalem had escaped the angel's sword in David's day (1 Chr. 21:26–27). Not only is this 'a place to make offerings' (2:6), it is also a place where offerings will be accepted.

The account of the temple's construction deliberately parallels the passages in Exodus dealing with the making of the tabernacle. The language of the two accounts is very similar, using the refrain '… and he made …' Solomon is presented as a new Bezalel. The Lord singled out both of them for their task by name (Exod. 31:1–2; 35:30; 1 Chr. 22:9–10; 28:6; 29:1), both were from the tribe of Judah (Exod. 31:2), and both were given wisdom specifically for their building tasks (Exod. 31:3; 35:31). Similarly, Huram-abi takes on the role filled by Oholiab back in Exodus. We are being reminded that there is an essential continuity between the tabernacle and the temple, while the increased measurements and additional items tell us that there is development as well. At the same time as the writer nods towards the tabernacle, he also gives David credit for the preparation of both skilled workers (2:7) and materials (5:1).

Roughly 1,000 years later, someone else was involved in a building project of sorts, and his mind turned to this part of God's Word. He thought of himself as 'a skilled master builder' (1 Cor. 3:10[1]) who had laid a foundation[2] for a different kind of temple. His foundation was the preaching of 'Christ crucified' (1 Cor. 1:23) and the temple he had in mind was a local church.[3] Just as Solomon needed the help of Huram-abi, Paul had 'fellow workers' (1 Cor. 3:9). Using a different picture, Paul had already described how he had 'planted, [and] Apollos watered' (1 Cor. 3:6). There would be others building on Paul's foundation as well as Apollos, and Paul, like Solomon, wanted the best materials to be used. Solomon didn't use just any old cedars; they had to be Lebanese (2 Chr. 2:8), and the gold had to be from Parvaim

(3:6). Paul's concern was that church-builders were 'not to go beyond what is written' (1 Cor. 4:6), but were to be trustworthy 'stewards of the mysteries of God' (1 Cor. 4:1). Not everyone is a 'master builder', but Paul made it clear to the Corinthians (and us) that we all have a responsibility to 'Let all things be done for building up' (1 Cor. 14:26). With the responsibility comes a wonderful promise. In light of the resurrection, whatever our particular contribution to the church of Jesus Christ, we can be 'steadfast, immovable, always abounding in the work of the Lord, knowing that in the Lord [our] labour is not in vain' (1 Cor. 15:58).

> Not everyone is a 'master builder', but Paul made it clear to the Corinthians (and us) that we all have a responsibility to 'Let all things be done for building up'.

The ark that Solomon brought (5:2–14)

While the account of the construction of the temple is modelled on the tabernacle account in Exodus, that of the transportation of the ark looks back to the parallel episode in David's reign. The temple on its own is really just a shell. It is to be a 'resting place' for the ark (Ps. 132:8, 14). The permanence of this move is underlined by Solomon's timing. The 'feast that is in the seventh month' (2 Chr. 5:3) is the feast of tabernacles—the feast that commemorated the wanderings in the wilderness and celebrated harvest. Here is a sign that the wanderings are over. The ark is coming home. The harvest is in. It is being brought 'to its place' (v. 7), where it belongs. No wonder that this 'triumphal entry' is accompanied by united 'praise and thanksgiving to the LORD' (v. 13). A symbol of the special presence of the Lord is being placed at the heart of Jerusalem, and the Lord himself is special: 'For he is good, for his steadfast love endures for ever' (v. 13).

Even with the ark in place, all is not yet ready. The temple is to be blessed with the reality which the ark merely represents (vv. 13–14). It had happened before in the tabernacle, in exactly the same way (Exod. 40:34). The Lord had said to Moses, 'make me a sanctuary, that I may dwell in their midst' (Exod. 25:8). The cloud was the visible sign that the Lord was moving in. The cloud seems to indicate that even this reality is, in some way, of necessity veiled. This is the Lord who 'dwells in unapproachable light' (1 Tim. 6:16), and yet who approaches his people—through the tabernacle, through the temple, and supremely through his Son. Even the glory of the Son of God was veiled during his earthly ministry (though with a partial glimpse on the mount of transfiguration). The book of Revelation tells us of the time when there will be no veil, and no cloud—when the new Jerusalem comes 'down out of heaven ... having the glory of God' (Rev. 21:10–11). There, we are told, we will see 'no temple in the city, for its temple is the Lord God'; and 'the city has no need of sun or moon ... for the glory of God gives it light' (Rev. 21:22–23).

That is something to look forward to, but what help is that right now? If you are reading this as a Christian, something wonderfully similar to what we read in 2 Chronicles 5 has happened to you. Certain weird and wonderful New Age philosophies claim that 'your body is a temple'. They usually mean that the physical body is to be treated with the utmost care and respect, perhaps even as sacred. As I write this, there is an advert on TV for a vitamin supplement which declares, 'Your body is a temple—worship it daily with _____.' Yet the Christian knows that there is greater truth in such a statement than many realize. When you turned from your sins and put your trust in the Lord Jesus, the Holy Spirit came to dwell within you (Rom. 8:9–11). The implications are staggering and sobering. It means that we have the same power at work within us to help us that raised the Saviour from the dead (Eph. 1:19–20; 3:20; 2 Tim. 1:14). It also means that we should be very careful what we do with our bodies, conscious that they now belong to God. It is only right that they should be devoted to him and his glory (1 Cor. 6:19–20). We are now temples, sanctified by the glory of God, just as the tabernacle and temple were (Exod. 29:43).

The prayer that Solomon prayed (6:1–42)

Solomon explains to the people what they are witnessing, much like Peter on the day of Pentecost. The essence of what Peter said was, '*This* is *that*': '*This* that is happening before your very eyes *is that* which was prophesied by Joel' (see Acts 2:16). And Solomon is effectively saying here, '*This* that is taking place in front of you now *is that* which the Lord promised to David' (2 Chr. 6:4, 10). He uses this memorable description about the God of Israel: that he 'with his hand has fulfilled what he promised with his mouth' (vv. 4, 15).

God's power matches his promises. We sometimes make promises that we prove unable to keep. Not so with the

Lord. When he says the word it's as good as done—in fact, sometimes his spoken word is seen to actually accomplish what is said (e.g. Gen. 1:3; Matt. 12:13).

Solomon begins his prayer by again acknowledging God's faithfulness in keeping part of his promise to David, before going on to ask that the Lord will keep the rest. It is reminiscent of the response of David himself to God's promise: 'let the word that you have spoken … be established … and do as you have spoken' (1 Chr. 17:23). Faith takes God at his word, while prayer reverently holds him to his word.

The story is told that, one day, as the Emperor Napoleon was reviewing some troops in Paris, he dropped his bridle and the horse bolted, with Napoleon clinging to the saddle. One of the rank-and-file soldiers sprang before the horse, seized the bridle and handed it to the emperor. Napoleon unthinkingly said, 'Much obliged to you, captain.' The quick-thinking soldier immediately took his chief at his word and asked, 'Of what regiment, sire?' Napoleon, impressed with the initiative of the young man, replied, 'Of my guards,' and galloped off. The emperor's word was his bond. Much more so with a God who is good, and whose 'steadfast love endures for ever' (2 Chr. 5:13).

> Faith takes God at his word, while prayer reverently holds him to his word.

Solomon's concern is that the Lord will be *actively* present at the temple, not just as a kind of religious mascot, but as a living God: there to hear prayer; there to forgive sin; there to act for his people. In his prayer he brings seven scenarios to the Lord (vv. 22–39) and asks that in all of these circumstances the Lord will hear, and/or forgive, and/or act in response to the pleas of his people. He is asking that the temple might be a place for the people to turn to in *all situations*.

It is also a prayer for *all times*. Centuries later, Daniel would go, three times a day, to his house, where 'he had windows in his upper chamber open towards Jerusalem' (Dan. 6:10). And if we were in any doubt what sorts of prayers he was praying, we are allowed to eavesdrop in chapter 9. What do we hear? We hear echoes of Solomon's prayer (see especially Dan. 9:17–19)—except that scenario number 7 of Solomon's prayer (2 Chr. 6:36–39) has now become a reality. Fast-forward about a century and we find Nehemiah praying, using Solomon's words as well (Neh. 1:6).

Solomon's prayer is a prayer for us, too. We are no longer focused on the temple as we pray; our focus is captured in the phrase 'in Jesus' name'. He is the answer to Solomon's question at 6:18 ('Will God indeed dwell with man on the earth?'), and he is all that the temple stood for (Matt. 12:6; John 2:19–21); the one in whom 'all the fullness of God was pleased to dwell' (Col. 1:19). And as we focus on him in prayer we can remember that he is seated on a 'throne of grace', where 'we may receive mercy and find grace to help in time of need' (Heb. 4:16).

Solomon makes clear what Jesus had to remind the people of his day: that the temple was to be 'a house of prayer' (Mark 11:17). Jesus was quoting Isaiah 56:7 and pointed out that the temple was also 'for *all the nations*' (my emphasis). That is something that also comes across from Solomon's prayer.

Scenario number 5 concerns 'a foreigner' and 'all the peoples of the earth' (2 Chr. 6:32–33). Jesus was angry that the court of the temple, designated for the Gentiles, had been turned into a Jewish market (and an extortionate one at that!). When God called Abram, it was so that 'all the families of the earth' should be blessed (Gen. 12:3). His purposes have never changed. It was because God so loved *the world* that, 'when the fullness of time had come' (Gal. 4:4), he 'gave his only Son, that *whoever* believes in him should not perish but have eternal life' (John 3:16).[4]

FOR FURTHER STUDY

1. Read Philippians 2:12–16. According to Paul in these verses, what will help us to shine in a dark world?

2. Read 1 Corinthians 6:12–20. What is Paul's specific concern here, and which more general principles does he outline?

3. Read Daniel 9:1–19. Which elements of Daniel's plea help us to know how to turn God's promises into prayer?

4. Read John 14:12–14; 16:22–24; 1 John 5:13–15. What does the phrase 'in Jesus' name' actually mean? Does it imply conditions concerning what we ask? (You could also look at Mark 9:37, 39; 13:6; 16:17.)

TO THINK ABOUT AND DISCUSS

1. What is your role in the ongoing building project of the church, and what are the right materials to use?

2. How can we build one another up?

3. What promises has God fulfilled in your own experience, and which ones are you still asking him to fulfil?

4. How does the New Testament answer Solomon's question in 2 Chronicles 6:18?

5. Come up with your own seven scenarios in which it would be especially helpful to keep in mind the need to pray. (If you are struggling, you could just try bringing the wording of Solomon's seven up to date for 21st-century Christians.)

3 One answer and a lot of questions

(7:1–9:31)

The offerings are accepted and Solomon's prayer is heard. Heard *and* answered. In detail. Even better, promises are given regarding the future, too. But there are searching conditions attached. The kingdom flourishes, and Solomon's fame spreads—all the way to Sheba.

Answered by fire (7:1–10)

Back in 1 Chronicles the Lord had demonstrated his acceptance of David's offerings in an unusual way. He 'answered him with fire' (1 Chr. 21:26). This had happened only once before, when worship at the tabernacle got underway. So we see a gracious God giving his visible stamp of approval to the offerings of the tabernacle, the location of the temple, and now the dedication of the temple (2 Chr. 7:1). The only other time we see the Lord answering by fire is at a similarly crucial point in Israel's history, when Elijah confronts the prophets of Baal on Mount Carmel (1 Kings 18:19–38). One day, a final offering, 'once for all' (Heb. 9:12, 26; 10:10), would be offered. On that occasion the sign of God's acceptance would be even more impressive than fire: resurrection!

In response to this awe-inspiring spectacle in Jerusalem we have another example of worship and thanksgiving, the summary of which is becoming familiar (2 Chr. 7:3). We have come across the refrain 'For he is good, for his steadfast love endures for ever' before in Chronicles (1 Chr. 16:34, 41; 2 Chr. 5:13). God's goodness and steadfast love is a recurring theme of Israel's praise in the Old Testament. The Hebrew term translated 'steadfast love' is closely related to the idea of a covenant. It is loyal love that expresses its commitment in the form of a solemn promise. Israel is rejoicing in the latest example of God's faithfulness in keeping his promises to Moses, David, Solomon and Israel (7:10).

Answered by promise (7:11–22)

Having demonstrated his acceptance of the offerings, the Lord appears to Solomon to give a specific assurance that his prayer has been heard. Not only has it been heard—the answer is a resounding 'Yes!' The only thing is that it is an answer with a lot of 'if's. The Lord's answer places the emphasis on those 'if's. There is the people's 'if' and then Solomon's 'if'. You'll have to read 1 Kings 11 to see how far short Solomon ultimately fell with his 'if's.

For the people, however, the 'if' concerns *how* they ask (v. 14). Will the people humble themselves as they pray? Will their praying involve a real seeking of the Lord himself? Will they turn from wickedness as they turn to the Lord?

'If' no. 1: Humbling ourselves

Pride comes naturally. It was the sin which got Satan thrown out of heaven and which played a key role in Adam and Eve being thrown out of Eden. We need to take time to humble ourselves.

A friend of President Roosevelt's told how, often, after an evening's talk, they would stroll outside and look up into the night sky. They would see who could first find the pale bit of light near the upper-left-hand corner of the Great Square of Pegasus. Then one of them would exclaim, 'That is the spiral galaxy of Andromeda! It is as large as our Milky Way. It is one of a hundred million galaxies. It is two and a half million light-years away. It consists of one hundred billion suns, many of them larger than our own sun!' After a moment of quiet, Roosevelt would grin and say, 'Now I think we are small enough. Let's go to bed!'[1]

I can't remember where I found it, but my favourite definition of pride is 'an inflated opinion of ourselves that we expect others to share'. We all need to learn the art of cutting ourselves down to size. True humility is not having a *deflated* but an *accurate* opinion of ourselves. And that doesn't mean accurate in comparison with others, but in comparison with God's standards. One of Winston Churchill's well-known witticisms was a cutting comment about one of his political opponents: 'Mr Attlee is a very modest man. Indeed he has a

> True humility is not having a *deflated* but an *accurate* opinion of ourselves.

lot to be modest about.'[2] The point is that we all have a lot to be modest about. It will do us good to remind ourselves of that frequently. Scripture multiplies blessings to the humble: they will be saved (2 Sam. 22:28); led and taught (Ps. 25:9); lifted up (Ps. 147:6); looked to (Isa. 66:2); and given grace (James 4:6; 1 Peter 5:5). On the other hand, there are many warnings for the proud.

A young man fresh out of theological college was excited about preaching his first sermon in his home church. As he was introduced, feeling fully prepared, he walked boldly to the pulpit, head held high, and radiating self-confidence. Soon, though, he was stumbling through the Scripture reading, and then he lost his train of thought half-way through the message. Beginning to panic, he quickly brought the sermon to an end and walked dejectedly, head down, from the pulpit. A wise elder gently spoke to him a little later: 'If you had gone up to the pulpit the way you came down, you might have come down the way you went up.'[3]

What will help us attain and maintain a healthy humility? A grasp of the glory and holiness of God will be a good start, preferably accompanied by a knowledge of our own weakness and sinfulness. As one of the Puritans put it, 'They that know God will be humble; they that know themselves cannot be proud.'[4] The only boasting permissible for the Christian is 'in the cross' (Gal. 6:14). If we spend time at the foot of the cross, thinking about all that our Saviour suffered and accomplished there, the effect is wonderful: we will 'pour contempt on all [our] pride'.[5]

'If' no. 2: Seeking his face

The idea of seeking is closely tied to prayer, here (v. 14) and elsewhere. Prayer is not just a matter of getting things said, or working through a kind of shopping list. We aren't supposed to be merely seeking positive answers to our prayers; we are to seek the face of God. Part of what that means is to seek an audience with the Lord (see 2 Sam. 3:13). We want our God to hear what we have got to say, but we also want to be in his presence. In fact, John Preston, a Puritan minister, wrote a whole book on 2 Chronicles 7:14 entitled *The Golden Sceptre Held Forth to the Humble*, viewing the verse as an encouragement to come into the 'inner court' of the Lord's presence, as illustrated in the story of Esther (Esth. 4:11).

To 'seek his face' also involves seeking the Lord's favour and blessing. Numerous times in Scripture we read of the Lord making 'his face shine' on his people (see Num. 6:25; Ps. 4:6; 31:16; 67:1; 80:3, 7, 19; 119:135), and this means that he is accepting them, looking upon them favourably, and is ready to do them good. We might say that they are enjoying God's 'smile'. That is a goal of true seeking. But there's something more. Seeking God's face also expresses real intimacy. It is said of Moses that 'there has not arisen a prophet since in Israel like Moses, whom the LORD knew face to face' (Deut. 34:10). Every Christian has seen something of 'the glory of God in the face of Jesus Christ', but we can all join in the prayer that we might 'see Christ more clearly, love him more dearly, and follow him more nearly'.[6] As we seek such intimacy we can be confident that we will one day 'find' in the fullest sense. 'For now we see in a mirror dimly, but then face to face. Now I know in part; then I shall know fully, even as I have been fully known' (1 Cor. 13:12).

Elsewhere in Scripture, 'seeking' can also be used to describe the desire for guidance, but in Chronicles this simple phrase is used most often as a kind of shorthand for true devotion to the Lord. We will see other elements of seeking highlighted in the lives of some of Judah's kings later on in Chronicles.

'If' no. 3: Turning from our wicked ways

Those who take the idea of seeking God seriously will be equally concerned with turning from their wicked ways. Seeking implies faith, and this 'turning' is what repentance is all about. Repentance and faith are two sides of the same coin. Repentance puts the emphasis on what you turn from: sin. Faith focuses on whom we turn to: God, especially as revealed in the person of Jesus Christ.

An American minister tells of how, as a boy, he found a discarded big, black cigar, which he duly attempted to smoke. Although it tasted pretty awful, it made him feel very grown-up and pleased with himself—until he saw his father approaching. He quickly put the cigar behind his back and tried to 'act casual'. In an attempt to divert his father's attention, he pointed to a poster advertising a circus that was in town. 'Can I go, Dad? Please, let's go when it comes to town.' His father's reply was quiet, firm and memorable: 'Son, never make a petition while at the same time trying to hide a smouldering disobedience.'[7] The psalmist had said much the same thing centuries before: 'If I had cherished iniquity in my heart, the Lord would not have listened' (Ps. 66:18). Solomon himself would record this principle in one of his proverbs: 'If one turns away his ear from hearing the law, even his prayer is an abomination' (Prov. 28:9).

True turning from sin has three aspects: past, present and future. Turning from sin in the past will be shown by real sadness, *regretting* what happened. Present turning from sin is an actual *renouncing of* (or rejecting) the particular sin in question with all of our being; not at some other time, but right now. Then, as we think about the future, we will be *resolving* to steer clear of the sin in the future. That will involve plans to avoid situations where temptation may strike and a determination to look out for warning signs in our own hearts and circumstances, so that we can be spiritually 'on our toes'.

> True turning from sin has three aspects: past, present and future.

If the people of Israel manage to fulfil these 'if's, they have a promise even better than the one Solomon is requesting. Not only will the Lord's 'eyes … be open' towards the temple, and his 'ears attentive' to the people's prayers, but his 'heart will … be there' as well (6:20; 7:15–16).

There are personal promises, personal 'if's and personal warnings for Solomon as well. The consequences of disobedience are vividly portrayed, as if the writer is concerned to vindicate God with regard to his future dealings with Israel, though not at all concerned to deal with Solomon's personal 'fall from grace'.

Solomon's work (8:1–18)

The focus of Chronicles is Solomon's accomplishments in his official capacity as king. Building projects are listed in this chapter, including the completion of *the* building project—the temple—and the setting up of regular worship there 'according to the commandment of Moses' (v. 13). Solomon's work, and especially the house of the Lord, is completed. He could have used the words that his greater descendant would use about a greater work nearly a thousand years later: 'I glorified you on earth, having accomplished the work that you gave me to do' (John 17:4). The temple is the crowning achievement of Solomon's reign, and the gold from Ophir (v. 18) underlines the glory of his kingdom.

The inquisitive queen (9:1–31)

Solomon's fame begins to spread and attracts the queen of Sheba, who is keen to see if his wisdom will live up to all the hype. She seems to have a lot in common with the apostle Thomas, who needed to see before he believed (see John 20:25). Peter could say to some early Christians, 'Though you have not seen [Christ], you love him. Though you do not now see him, you believe in him and rejoice with joy' (1 Peter 1:8). That was a measure of these Christians' faith. Like Thomas, however, the queen of Sheba has some doubt mixed with her faith. Her response to the report that she has heard—travelling many miles—shows some faith, but she admits to significant doubt as well (9:6). Seeing is believing for the queen, who goes on to make a similar confession to that of Hiram (v. 8; compare 2:12). The Lord Jesus commended her for travelling 'from the ends of the earth' to hear the wisdom of Solomon (Matt. 12:42), in contrast to the scribes and Pharisees, who weren't interested in hearing the wisdom of the Saviour. All they wanted was a sign, when what they needed to do was believe.

From 9:13 to 9:21 a picture of the magnificence of Solomon's court is painted for us, and it is then plainly stated that he 'excelled all the kings of the earth in riches and in wisdom' (v. 22). Only one king who followed would surpass him, and he doesn't feature in 2 Chronicles. We need to turn to the New Testament to read of him: 'Christ, in whom are hidden all the treasures of wisdom and knowledge' (Col. 2:2–3).

FOR FURTHER STUDY

1. Read 1 Kings 18:19–38. What was the purpose of the confrontation, and what was the significance of the Lord's answering by fire?

2. Read 1 Kings 11:1–14. Why did Solomon turn away, and what made his sin worse?

3. Read Philippians 3:7–16. What can we learn from Paul in this passage about seeking God?

4. Read John 14:8–14. How might this passage help us in seeking God's face?

5. Read Psalm 51. Can you identify the verses in the psalm that correspond to the three 'if's? Are there any other lessons from the psalm about how to seek God?

TO THINK ABOUT AND DISCUSS

1. What have you got to be modest about?

2. What is there about the cross that we are to boast about, and what would such a boast sound like?

3. How might we be able to tell when we are 'enjoying God's smile', and how might we be mistaken?

4. Of the three aspects of 'turning' mentioned (past, present and future), which do you think is most difficult, and why?

5. If, having turned from sin, we go on to commit the same sin again, does that necessarily mean that our repentance was false? What might reassure us?

Part 2
The kingdom of Judah

4 The king who didn't set his heart to seek the Lord

(10:1–12:16)

Rehoboam's reign was like the proverbial curate's egg: good in parts. But just as an egg that is only good in parts really amounts to a bad egg, the final verdict on his reign is a solemn one: 'He did not set his heart to seek the LORD' (12:14).

Seeing a life summed up in a sentence certainly makes us think. It's no bad thing to live our lives with that kind of perspective. Scripture, though, actually encourages us to aim for something even more searching: an eternal perspective.

Abandoning the right advice (10:1–19)

We saw how Solomon set the tone for his reign by gathering 'all Israel' (1:2) to offer burnt offerings to the Lord. Now Rehoboam needs to decide on a statement of intent as his rule gets underway (vv. 1–6). Hindsight, of course, is a wonderful thing, and it is easy to criticize his adoption of a hard-line policy (v. 14), but there was a genuine decision to be made in these verses. Had a 'softly, softly' approach subsequently gone wrong, it would have been easy to castigate him for that with equal force. Just like his kingship as a whole, this particular incident is a real mixture of good and bad. His father's advice on wide consultation seems to have got through (vv. 6–9; assuming Solomon's authorship of Prov. 11:14; 15:22), but warnings about harshness and insolence went unheeded (see Prov. 1:10; 15:1). His man-management and people skills left a lot to be desired.

The writer of Chronicles, though, is at pains to point out that a different proverb is being illustrated here: 'The king's heart is a stream of water in the hand of the LORD; he turns it wherever he will' (Prov. 21:1). Why didn't Rehoboam listen to the people? Because it was 'a turn of affairs brought about by God that the LORD might fulfil his word' (2 Chr. 10:15; see 1 Kings 11:30–37). God was, and is, in control.

Even at a time that, historically, must have been viewed as tragic, with the kingdom about to be divided, the Lord's purposes were being worked out. That would have been a huge encouragement to the first readers of Chronicles. They were endeavouring to recover from a similar historic blow in the form of captivity in Babylon. To be reminded that their God was sovereignly ordering such events would have been tremendously reassuring. Not that Rehoboam bore no responsibility for this sad turn of affairs. The sovereignty of God and the responsibility of man are both clearly taught in Scripture as complementary rather than contradictory truths. As the great 19th-century preacher C. H. Spurgeon wisely put it in one of his sermons, '"How", says someone, "do you reconcile these two doctrines?" My dear brethren, I never reconcile two friends, never. These two doctrines are friends with one another; for they are both in God's Word, and I shall not attempt to reconcile them.'[1]

So the people rebel (10:16–18). And the writer wants us to be clear that, whatever failings Rehoboam has, this is rebellion 'against the house of David' (v. 19). They even use the same wording to declare independence that Sheba used in David's day. Sheba's was the cry of 'a worthless man' (2 Sam. 20:1), whereas a man whom, we are told, 'the Spirit clothed' had said just the opposite: 'We are yours, O David, and with you, O son of Jesse!' (1 Chr. 12:18).

> The sovereignty of God and the responsibility of man are both clearly taught in Scripture as complementary rather than contradictory truths.

Rehoboam doesn't realize just how final the split in his kingdom is. It takes the death of Hadoram (2 Chr. 10:18) to alert him to the reality and depth of the rebellion.

Abandoning the wrong plan (11:1–23)

Rehoboam isn't going to let the northern tribes go without a fight, but then 'the word of the LORD' comes to him, via Shemaiah, telling him to do just that. 'This thing is from me,' he says (v. 4). So Rehoboam finally recognizes when to give up. It is a shame for Hadoram that the lesson wasn't learnt that little bit sooner. But then it is a difficult lesson to learn. The TV show *Dragons' Den* has entrepreneurs pitching products to very wealthy potential investors. Regularly the 'dragons' plead with those making their pitch not to put any more money into a business that is clearly doomed. It can be quite comical (though tragic at the same time) to see the groundless confidence some of these inventors or innovators have in their products. They do not know when to cut their losses and recognize that their dreams are never going to materialize.

We are often encouraged to follow the example of Robert the Bruce, who, according to legend, learned from a spider that 'If at first you don't succeed, try, try and try again'. Persistence and perseverance are generally considered noble and heroic, and they undoubtedly often are. But sometimes closed doors are from God and submission is the order of the day. When the word of the Lord comes, the only thing to do is to listen and then respond positively. We will need to read our Bibles with our spiritual antennae up in case we, like Rehoboam, are in danger of barking up the wrong tree in our Christian lives. After all, even the apostle Paul needed a word from the Lord before he understood that persevering prayer about his 'thorn ... in the flesh' (2 Cor. 12:7–10) should give way to dependent acceptance.

Rehoboam's positive response to the word of the Lord results in a period of strengthening and security for the kingdom of Judah (vv. 5–12). One source of strength is of particular interest to the writer, whose concern for pure worship is so intense. Chronicles doesn't really cover the history of the northern kingdom, but continues to refer to 'all Israel' while making it clear that Judah is where David's line and true worship are preserved. In verses 13–17, because of its effect on the south under Rehoboam, there is just a passing reference to Jeroboam's departure from the worship of the Lord. The Levites in the north are suddenly out of a job. As Jeroboam sets up his own national religion to serve his own purposes, the Levites head for Jerusalem (v. 14). More importantly, they are not alone. They are joined by others 'from all the tribes of Israel' (v. 16).

Here was a wonderful example for the first readers of Chronicles to be inspired by. This was the way that they could hope to re-establish the kingdom and temple worship in Jerusalem. Help from 'all Israel' would be essential, and it would have to come from people of a high spiritual calibre. The quality needed is summed up in a key phrase that describes these people: they 'set their hearts to seek the LORD God of Israel' (v. 16). Rehoboam didn't (12:14). How about you?

These people had a heart for the true worship of the true God, and they were prepared to take risks and endure hardships accordingly. They knew that acceptable worship of the Lord was founded upon sacrifice (11:16), and they also knew their God. He was 'the God of their fathers', who had been gracious and faithful to Abraham, Isaac, Jacob, Joseph, Moses, Joshua ... and right down to the days of David, Solomon and now Rehoboam. Jeroboam could change his gods (1 Kings 12:28–31), but these people were sticking with their unchanging God. Jeroboam's loss was Rehoboam's gain (2 Chr. 11:17).

There is a decisiveness and resolve, a firm intent, about their seeking of the Lord. It is reminiscent of Ruth's determination to follow Naomi in the days of the judges. I like the wording of the King James Version in Ruth 1:18, when it says that Ruth was 'stedfastly minded'. It is no surprise that such people 'strengthened the kingdom' (2 Chr. 11:17). Such people strengthen the church of Jesus Christ, too.

Three golden years follow, accompanied by some uncharacteristically wise administration (v. 23); all of this blessing is seen to have its source in Rehoboam's positive response to 'the word of the LORD' (v. 4). This happy period harks back to the glory days of David and Solomon.

Abandoning the law (12:1–5)

Disappointingly, what follows resembles not the reigns of David and Solomon, but that of Saul. A phrase that was used to sum up where Saul went wrong is used of Rehoboam in these verses: he, and all Israel with him, was 'unfaithful to', or 'broke faith with', the Lord (v. 2; compare 1 Chr. 10:13²). This is the phrase that Chronicles uses to sum up the biggest mistake anyone can make (see also 1 Chr. 2:7; 9:1). There is a sense of déjà vu about chapter 12. We have seen Rehoboam make a serious mistake and then partially recover in chapters 10 and 11, and we go through the same cycle again here in chapter 12. He didn't know how to handle power at the beginning of his reign, and he doesn't know how to handle the position of strength he finds himself in at the beginning of chapter 12.

Sometimes in our lives we reach points where we can recognize that, in some sense, 'we've been here before'. We'll need to have learned from our mistakes a whole lot more effectively than Rehoboam did. We will see from a number of Judah's kings that a position of strength can be a position of danger, while an experience of weakness can lead to a wonderful deliverance.

Saul's error was further explained as a failure to 'keep the command of the LORD' (1 Chr. 10:13), and what Rehoboam got wrong was that 'he abandoned the law of the LORD' (2 Chr. 12:1). The Bible knows of no way of following the Lord that doesn't involve straightforward obedience. If we love the Lord Jesus, we will keep his commandments (John 14:15). The law and the Lord are inseparable. When someone abandons the law, the Lord declares, 'You abandoned me' (2 Chr. 12:5).

The sequel really is a sequel: it is no coincidence that Shishak and his army subsequently take 'the fortified cities of Judah' (v. 4) and arrive at Jerusalem. There is a causal link—God is sovereign over Shishak and Egypt, as well as over Rehoboam and Judah. While trouble doesn't always follow sin as a direct result—the Lord Jesus warns us against making such assumptions (John 9:3)—it sometimes does, and this is one of those times. Lest Rehoboam miss the connection, the Lord sends Shemaiah the prophet to leave him in no doubt that this invasion is a piece of divine justice (2 Chr. 12:5). Our God is a God who is just. Thankfully, it is also true that 'his mercy is very great' (1 Chr. 21:13). Even as he pronounces judgements he 'waits to be gracious' (Isa.

> The Bible knows of no way of following the Lord that doesn't involve straightforward obedience.

30:18—see the whole verse). It's as if the Lord is looking for almost any excuse to be gracious rather than merely just. The sending of a prophet is itself an act of mercy, and even when the message is one of condemnation there is an implied offer of mercy. That was spelled out in Jeremiah's day: 'If at any time I declare concerning a nation or a kingdom, that I will pluck up and break down and destroy it, and if that nation, concerning which I have spoken, turns from its evil, I will relent of the disaster that I intended to do to it' (Jer. 18:7–8).

Abandoning pride (12:6–16)

Happily, confronted by a prophet for the second time, Rehoboam responds positively again. Reacting well to the word of the Lord is always a good move. In 2 Chronicles we see bad kings reacting badly to prophets and good kings reacting well to them. Perhaps more interestingly, we see bad kings reacting well, and good kings reacting badly. 'Even the bad benefit from listening to the Lord's prophets, and the good will still suffer when they don't—so LISTEN and LEARN!' is the lesson that is being hammered home.

Prophets were usually raised up when God's people needed confronting, and when we are confronted there are only two ways we can go: proud rejection or humble acceptance. With Shemaiah's message ringing in his ears, Rehoboam abandons the pride that seemed to be a feature of his handling of Jeroboam at the beginning of his reign. What he says is, 'The LORD is righteous', but what he is doing is humbling himself (v. 6). He is taking sides with God against himself: 'You're right and I'm wrong', or, more generally, 'You're in the right, and I'm in the wrong'. The ease with which you admit you are wrong will tell you how humble you are.

Judah had at least fulfilled one of the conditions stipulated by the Lord back in 7:14. Rehoboam never gets to seeking the Lord or turning from his wicked ways (12:14), but some humbling brings 'some deliverance' (v. 7). Humbling yourself is something else that is always a good move. Something good in his conduct leads to some 'good in Judah' (v. 12).

Nevertheless, there is a 'nevertheless' involved (v. 8). Bob Dylan famously sang, 'You gotta serve somebody.' The only question is, who will it be? Refusing to serve the Lord will involve serving a much harder taskmaster, but some people insist on learning the hard way. Moses had warned, many years before, that those who 'did not serve the LORD … with joyfulness and gladness of heart' would 'serve [their] enemies' instead (Deut. 28:47–48). Many years later, the Lord Jesus made a similar appeal to us to take his yoke upon us, with the assurance that his yoke 'is easy' (Matt. 11:29–30). To be 'appointed to his service' (see 1 Tim. 1:12) is a cause for thanksgiving, and to be his 'servant' (Rom. 1:1) is a position of the highest honour.

It won't be the last time that what happens to the temple under a particular king will prove to be a commentary on his entire reign. The shields of gold are exchanged for shields of bronze (12:9–10), and a glorious kingdom becomes distinctly third class. Solomon's gold has been tarnished, and all for the want of a set heart.

For further study ▶

FOR FURTHER STUDY

1. Read 2 Corinthians 4:16–18; Romans 8:18; and 2 Timothy 4. How will an eternal perspective help us, and what can we do to cultivate one?

2. Read Matthew 11:15 and 13:10–17, 43. What are the implications of what the Lord says here?

3. Read Matthew 18:7 and Acts 2:23. Can you see how these verses handle God's sovereignty and human responsibility? What is clear, and what is left unexplained? (Study Rom. 9:14–24 if you would like to explore this further.)

4. Read 2 Corinthians 12:7–10. How did the Lord help Paul to accept the situation, and what did Paul learn as a result?

5. Read 1 Corinthians 11:27–32. What was the sin here that was the direct cause of sickness and even death? What advice does Paul give us on how to avoid such discipline, and what does he say is its purpose?

6. Read Matthew 6:24 and Romans 6:12–14. Which different masters are in view here? What sort of things will we need to do to obey Paul, and how does he encourage us?

TO THINK ABOUT AND DISCUSS

1. What are the best sources of advice you can turn to when a difficult decision needs to be made?

2. What steps can we take to help us listen to, and act upon, God's Word?

3. What principles may help us to recognize when we should persevere with something and when it is time to accept that we should give up?

4. Can you remember a time when you could say that you 'set your heart' to do something? How did that affect your life at the time? What might deflect us from seeking the Lord?

5 The preaching king and the afflicted king

(13:1–16:14)

Abijah's reign is of interest chiefly because of a military clash highlighting the importance of crying to and relying upon the Lord. Asa models the same principle when he takes the throne, only for his reign to end on a sour and sad note.

Abijah's sermon (13:1–12)

Abijah's three-year reign receives little attention in 1 Kings (where he is known as Abijam). We are told that 'his heart was not wholly true to the Lord his God' (1 Kings 15:3). His son and heir, Asa, fares better by this crucial measure; despite his failings and falterings, his heart 'was wholly true to the Lord all his days' (1 Kings 15:14). The writer of Kings can find nothing positive to say about Abijah himself. The only good thing to say about him is that he is descended from David, but that is good enough for him to enjoy some measure of blessing from God, 'for David's sake' (15:3–4). He doesn't deserve it, but his connection with David means that he receives it nonetheless.

This is a helpful reminder of why we might use the phrase 'for Jesus' sake' in our prayers. We are conscious (in a way that Abijah showed no sign of grasping) that we don't deserve our prayers to be heard, or to receive the blessings we seek, but it is our connection with God's beloved Son, 'with whom [He is] well pleased' (Matt. 3:17), that enables us to make our requests with boldness and confidence.

> It is our connection with God's beloved Son, 'with whom [He is] well pleased', that enables us to make our requests with boldness and confidence.

Like Kings, Chronicles doesn't have much to say about Abijah's reign, and nothing about his heart. Abijah's little sermon to Jeroboam, on the other hand, and its aftermath, does have a key lesson for Israel, Judah and us. Abijah's words are better than his heart. Knowing what we do about him from 1 Kings, his sermon in 1 Chronicles 13:4–12 takes on a distinct tinge of self-righteousness and self-satisfaction. Nevertheless, what he says is to the point, and is close to the heart of the writer as well.

Abijah reminds Jeroboam that God's covenant with David is still in full force and has not passed its sell-by date (v. 5). That is the significance of the phrase 'a covenant of salt', referring to the use of salt as a preservative.

For Jeroboam to go his own separate way from Judah, even allowing for Rehoboam's naivety, is to forsake the Lord (v. 11). And to then wage war on Judah is to 'withstand the kingdom of the LORD' (v. 8). Even when you outnumber your enemy two-to-one, if you are fighting 'against the LORD … you cannot succeed', Ahijah tells Jeroboam (v. 11).

Centuries later, an influential Jewish rabbi was conscious of the same danger Jeroboam was being warned about here—of unwittingly 'opposing God'. On that occasion the council 'took his advice' (Acts 5:39). But Jeroboam had made his choice. He might not have fully grasped the implications of what he was doing, but he was now at the point of no return. Superior numbers and cunning military strategy, however, are no match for God.

Judah's cry (13:13–22)

While Jeroboam gets things horribly wrong, the writer is careful to make clear that it is not Ahijah but Judah collectively who get things right. The king has a firm commitment to religious orthodoxy. What he doesn't have, however, is a prayerful reliance on the Lord. The men of Judah cry to God as they rely on God (v. 14). Back in 1 Chronicles 5, the two and a half tribes had cried out to God in battle and been helped 'because they trusted in him' (1 Chr. 5:20). Asa, Jehoshaphat, Hezekiah and Isaiah would follow suit in due course (2 Chr. 14:11; 18:31; 32:20). Here was one of the scenarios Solomon had envisaged as he prayed at the dedication of the temple, and the Lord did indeed 'hear from heaven … and maintain their cause', just as he had asked (6:35).

While Abijah doesn't get any of the credit for this episode, he does get some of the benefit. He 'grew mighty' while Jeroboam grew weak (13:20–21). Relying on the Lord and rebelling against the Lord have very different consequences. Rebels are ultimately 'subdued'; reliers 'prevail' (v. 18).

Asa's work of reformation (14:1–8)

While Abijah is a somewhat ambiguous figure in Chronicles, the writer doesn't leave us in any doubt about Asa. Lest the closing scenes of his life mislead us, we are told at the outset that here was a king who 'did what was good and right in the eyes of the LORD his God' (14:2). And he does a lot. He presides over a fairly thorough religious reformation, as well as an extensive building and fortification programme. The heart of Asa's reformation is the command 'to seek the LORD' (v. 4), and the basis of the peace he enjoys in the early years of his reign is Judah's positive response (v. 7). In the process, Asa taught Judah, and teaches us, that seeking the Lord is closely allied to keeping 'the law and the commandment' (v. 4).

Asa's cry (14:9–15)

When on the brink of war, in contrast to Abijah's day, this time it is the king himself who cries to the Lord. Not just any Lord, but 'the LORD *his* God' (v. 11). Asa knows his God, and his prayer reinforces that fact. He knows that his God is unique, is able to help the weak, and that his God is 'our God'—the God of Judah. The Lord had said that Israel were called by his name (7:14), so when they went into battle, they could rightly say that they were engaging the enemy in his name. His reputation was at stake. And for Asa, knowing the character of his God makes it second nature to rely on him. As the psalmist said, '… those who know your name put their trust in you' (Ps. 9:10).

When J. G. Paton, missionary to the South Seas, was translating the Scriptures for the islanders, for a long time he just could not find any word in their language that adequately translated the word 'believe'. One day, one of the locals came into his study exhausted, flung himself down on a chair, rested his feet on another chair and stretched out, saying how good it was to lean his whole weight on those chairs. Instantly Paton knew he had his word for 'believe'.[1] When you trust someone, you are prepared to lean your whole weight on that person's word. To lean your whole weight on the word of another is what faith is all about. Here Asa leans his whole weight on what he knows his God is like. The word 'rely' (v. 11) is an important one in Chronicles, and it will prove to be especially significant in the life of Asa.

Azariah's prophecy (15:1–7)

The Bible is full of encouragements, and the Lord now sends a prophet to literally 'en-courage' (i.e. 'put courage into') Asa. We might be inclined to think that courage is most needed for going into battle, but the Bible often talks about the need for courage simply in order to do what is right. The danger Azariah warns against is that of our hands being weakened (v. 7).

> To lean your whole weight on the word of another is what faith is all about.

How did Nehemiah pray when he encountered hostility as he set about rebuilding the walls of Jerusalem? 'But now, O God, strengthen my hands' (Neh. 6:9). Opposition tends to have a draining effect. So can the Lord's discipline, as the writer of Hebrews was aware: 'Therefore lift your drooping hands' (Heb. 12:12). Those who do what is right usually meet resistance: sometimes from the world, other times from the sin that lurks within, or even from the devil and his minions.

The story is told of a time when the devil decided to sell some of his tools. The day of the sale arrived and there were many chilling implements on display with high price tags attached. Pride, hatred, jealousy and anger were all expensive items, with many more besides. As the doors were opened and prospective buyers looked around, one of them noticed a relatively small, well-worn object to one side with a sign next to it reading, 'Not for sale'. He asked the devil about it and got the reply, 'That is a tool I cannot do without. It is *discouragement*, and it can get into the hearts of men and women where my other tools are powerless. Once inside I can really get to work. It is my most effective tool and the best thing is that few people know that it belongs to me.'[2]

How, then, does Azariah help us to fight discouragement? In three ways: with a principle, a warning and a promise. Sometimes we become discouraged when we feel that we are on our own (ask Elijah—1 Kings 18:22; 19:10, 14) but, says Azariah, we can be sure of the principle that *the Lord is with us* while we are with him (15:2). He also warns us that giving way to discouragement could prove to be a slippery slope towards forsaking the Lord (v. 2). A *consideration of the consequences* of our actions can stop us in our tracks when nothing else will.

Another cause of discouragement comes when we ask ourselves if there is any point—to our lives, or to what we are doing at any given time (ask Solomon—Eccles. 1:2–3, 14; 2:1, 11, 15, 17, 19, 21, 23, 26, etc.). That's why the Bible—and the Lord Jesus—have a lot to say about rewards. There is nothing wrong with being motivated by *the promise of a reward*. Actually, when the promise comes from God, you will need faith to be motivated by it. Azariah assures Asa that his 'work shall be rewarded' (15:7). Jesus assures us that 'whoever gives one of these ... even a cup of cold water because he is a disciple ... will by no means lose his reward' (Matt. 10:42). Paul gives us the same assurance with the added explanation of how we can be so sure: the resurrection! He brings his great teaching on the resurrection to a conclusion with the same encouragement that Azariah brings to Asa: 'Therefore ... be steadfast, immovable, always abounding in the work of the Lord, knowing that in the Lord your labour is not in vain' (1 Cor. 15:58).

Asa's work of renewal (15:8–19)

Knowing that his work will be rewarded, Asa takes courage (v. 8) and duly does abound in the work of the Lord. It must take great boldness to remove the idols from the land, but the real measure of his courage, one suspects, is removing Maacah, his mother, from her official position as queen mother (v. 16). Azariah's principle holds good: the Lord *is* with him—so much so that it is evident to others (v. 9), who join the southern kingdom from Israel as a result. Temple repairs (v. 8) are a good sign in any reign, and the fact that they are followed by a national gathering where the people enter into a covenant (vv. 9–15) marks this out as a high point in Judah's history. We won't see a gathering quite like this again until we reach the time of Josiah (34:29–33). At the heart of the covenant is the theme at the heart of Chronicles: seeking the Lord. And there is no doubt that they are in earnest. The seeking they are intent on is 'with all their heart and with all their soul' (15:12). That they take this seriously is made even clearer by the ultimate penalty for the uncommitted (v. 13). It reminds us that we are all faced with a stark choice. We can seek or we can forsake, but there is no middle ground. 'Whoever is not with me', says the Lord Jesus, 'is against me' (Matt. 12:30). Whenever we hear the Word of the Lord there is a choice to be made, and, as Moses makes clear, that boils down to a choice between life and death (Deut. 30:19). The sanction may seem dramatic, but it really only makes the inevitable consequence of the choice more immediate.

> Whenever we hear the Word of the Lord there is a choice to be made, and, as Moses makes clear, that boils down to a choice between life and death.

Azariah's promise is fulfilled here as well: they seek, and the Lord is found. Nor do they have to wait very long for his further promise of reward to be realized: 'the LORD gave them rest all round' (v. 15). We may have to wait a good deal longer.

Much has been accomplished, even if some high places in Israel survive (v. 17), and Asa's heart is in the right place—as his attention to the temple demonstrates (v. 18).

Asa's foolish covenant (16:1–14)

Up to this point Asa has been an excellent example for us

all to learn from and imitate. Sadly the close of his reign serves as a cautionary tale. We have already learned how to rely on the Lord and how to respond to a prophet from the Lord. It just makes it all the more tragic that we learn the very opposite from the same man. In some ways it is easier to rely on the Lord when he is your only hope in a desperate situation. Paul wrote to the Corinthians of how he had felt, at one point in his missionary journeys, that he 'had received the sentence of death. But that was to make us rely not on ourselves but on God who raises the dead' (2 Cor. 1:9). What proves to be Asa's undoing when under threat from Baasha king of Israel is that a possible way out of the situation presents itself to him. It's a test, and Asa fails it. To break Baasha's blockade, Asa raids the temple and relies on the king of Syria for help (vv. 1–3). Underlining the contrast between Asa's conduct here and earlier, the writer records that Asa enters into a second 'covenant'. This one is with Ben-hadad king of Syria, not the Lord, and it involves Ben-hadad breaking his covenant with Baasha. Doesn't Asa see the intrinsic unreliability of a covenant with a king who is willing to break another covenant at the drop of a hat (or some temple treasures)? Apparently not. He may be too busy congratulating himself on such a successful diplomatic manoeuvre, because everything has gone according to plan. Until Hanani arrives.

'You could and should have relied on me this time as well,' is the Lord's message (vv. 7–9). Then Asa would be relying on a God who is ready 'to give strong support to those whose heart is blameless towards him' (v. 9). Asa's response to being confronted by Hanani is to fly into a rage and put him in the prison stocks (v. 10). Wars, cruelty and disease follow. And his reaction to the disease is no better than his reaction to Baasha's threat. In fact, it is worse, because the disease 'became severe' and he still did not seek the Lord but simply relied on physicians (v. 12).

There doesn't have to be an either/or choice between the Lord and medicine—usually it is a case of both/and. The Lord generally uses means to bring about recovery; we just need to be careful not to rely on the means themselves. At least we have the writer's assurance that 'the heart of Asa was wholly true all his days' (15:17), otherwise we might well have had our doubts. So Asa is worthy of honour, but those final five years meant that his reign and reputation rather lost their lustre. Asa was the loser for not relying on the Lord and not responding to his word—and so will we be if we repeat his mistakes.

FOR FURTHER STUDY

1. Read Matthew 16:21–23. What is so serious about Peter's mistake? How did he come to be opposing God without meaning to?

2. Read 2 Corinthians 4–5. What antidotes to discouragement does Paul come up with in this passage (note 4:1; 4:16; 5:6)?

3. Read Hebrews 12:3–11. What causes of discouragement are dealt with in this passage, and what help is there for dealing with it?

4. Read Hebrews 11:23–28 and 12:1–2. How did the prospect of a reward help Moses and Jesus? What aspect of the reward did they focus on?

TO THINK ABOUT AND DISCUSS

1. What causes of discouragement do you struggle with most?

2. Can you think of a time when you felt the need for courage before doing what was right?

3. What do you think might be the equivalent of high places in the modern Christian church (i.e. things that are wrong but never seem to be dealt with or recognized as wrong)? And in your own Christian life?

4. What things are we sometimes tempted to rely on instead of the Lord?

5. Have you ever been angry with someone who has reproved you in some way, only to recognize later that he or she was right? Have you seen others react like this?

6 The courageous king, the unloved king and the wicked king

(17:1–22:12)

Jehoshaphat is a bit of an enigma. He is undoubtedly one of the best kings of Judah, yet he is a flawed king. For all his fine qualities, the account of Jehoshaphat's reign is a tale of two battles in which we see him at his compromised worst and prayerful best.

Growing greatness (17:1–19)

The writer, introducing Jehoshaphat, is at pains to say, 'Now, before we get to the Ahab episode, I want you to be quite clear that this king was a good man. Was the Lord with him? Check. Did he walk in the ways of David? Check. Did he seek God? Check. Don't think he was a coward—his "heart was courageous in the ways of the LORD" [v. 6].' As well as his personal qualities we see a wise and godly domestic policy adopted for instructing the people of Judah in 'the Law of the LORD' (v. 9). His international standing is also secure, chiefly because 'the fear of the LORD fell upon all the kingdoms of the lands that were around Judah' (v. 10). The army of Judah is at its strongest. From numbering 180,000 in the days of Rehoboam (11:1) to 400,000 under Abijah (13:3) and 580,000 under Asa (14:8), it reaches over a million here. King and kingdom seem to be in good shape. Part of the reason for recording Judah's military strength may well be to underline just how unnecessary it was to join forces with the north.

An alarming alliance (18:1–19:3)

From a position of riches and strength Jehoshaphat makes a poor and weak decision. The writer seems to suggest a connection between Jehoshaphat's riches and honour and the marriage alliance with Ahab (v. 1). His position may well have attracted an offer from Ahab, but it is made clear that the marriage is Jehoshaphat's responsibility. It is a mistake that has unforeseen consequences. It leads to a subsequent visit with the in-laws. The phrase 'After some years' (v. 2) may well indicate a reluctance on Jehoshaphat's part. He may have put off the diplomatic visit numerous times until he felt unable to postpone it any longer. There is clearly further reluctance as he heads down the slippery slope to battle at Ramoth-gilead. The translation 'induced' (v. 2) is a fair one and suggests that Jehoshaphat has some qualms to overcome regarding Ahab's proposal. Then there is the recognition that none of Ahab's 'in-house' prophets are satisfactory and that another prophet needs to be consulted (v. 6), which clearly gives Jehoshaphat pause for thought. His discomfort is also evident when Ahab speaks contemptuously of the one genuine prophet available (v. 7). Jehoshaphat is sounding like someone who wishes he was somewhere else but who feels that it is too late to back out. And his silence is deafening as Ahab and Zedekiah mock and mistreat Micaiah. Jehoshaphat must be experiencing inner turmoil. He cannot shrug off Micaiah's message of impending doom (vv. 16–22) anything like as easily as Ahab can.

He probably smells a rat as Ahab explains his cunning plan to disguise himself while insisting that Jehoshaphat wear his royal robes (v. 29), but by this point Jehoshaphat seems to be resigning himself to the fact that his hands are tied. Judah's king has backed himself into a corner. Jehoshaphat has got in far too deep, but, 'out of the depths' (Ps. 130:1), he has the good sense to cry to the Lord (2 Chr. 18:31). God's promise to hear such cries extends even to situations that are our own silly fault. No situation is too desperate for us to experience the help of the Lord. But equally, as Ahab is to discover, no plan is cunning enough to escape the judgement of God.

Somerset Maugham retold the traditional story of a merchant in Baghdad who one day sent his servant to the market. His servant returned terrified, telling of how he had been jostled by Death at the market, who had made a threatening gesture towards him. The servant asked to borrow his master's horse so that he could flee to Samarra, and off he galloped. The merchant then headed to the market, found Death, and asked the reason for intimidating his servant. 'That was not a threatening gesture,' Death replied, 'it was only a start of surprise. I was astonished to see him in Baghdad, for I had an appointment with him tonight in Samarra.'[1] In Ahab's case, the bow drawn 'at random' (18:33) is appointed *by* the Lord, and Ahab has an inescapable appointment *with* the Lord.

Jehoshaphat doesn't know it but he has an appointment with a prophet on his safe return to Jerusalem. The whole sorry episode at Ramoth-gilead cannot simply be brushed under the carpet. The king needs to be challenged: 'What on earth do you think you've been doing? Well, I'll tell you what you've been doing: you have been helping the wicked and loving those who hate the Lord' (see 19:2). That is the truth of the whole episode in a nutshell.

The New Testament issues many similar warnings against alliances with false teachers. There should be no fellowship between believers and those who preach 'a different gospel' (Gal. 1:6–9). Those whom Paul describes as 'enemies of the cross of Christ' should not be our friends (Phil. 3:18). The apostle John is similarly clear about the seriousness of error when he says that we are not to offer hospitality or any sort of greeting to those who perpetuate such error, because 'whoever greets him takes part in his wicked works' (2 John 1:10–11). Has John forgotten that he is supposed to be 'the apostle of love'? No; it's just that love sometimes has to be tough. Tolerating serious error (or sin, for that matter) isn't loving; confronting those who teach it with the gravity of their situation is.

Thankfully, in Jehoshaphat's case, there is a 'nevertheless' to add before the prophet gives a complete picture of the situation. Not only does the Lord's prophet immediately get to the heart of recent events, he also reads the heart of the king. Happily there is 'some good' there—a determination 'to seek God' (19:3).

Good government (19:4–11)

There is a good response from this good heart to the prophet's reproof—and not a trace of the anger Asa displayed a few years earlier. Instead of turning away from the Lord himself, Jehoshaphat labours to turn the people back to the Lord. He appoints judges and priests who are given careful instructions about how to perform their duties.

Interestingly, the apostle Paul advocates the same approach to our duties. Fear of the Lord (2 Cor. 7:1; 1 Peter 2:17), carefulness (Eph. 5:15), impartiality (James 2:1, 9; 3:17; 1 Tim. 5:21), faithfulness (Gal. 5:22; 1 Tim. 3:11), wholeheartedness (Eph. 5:19; 6:5–6; 1 Tim. 1:5; 2 Tim. 2:22; 1 Peter 1:22), uprightness (Titus 1:8; 2:12) and courage (Acts 23:11; Eph. 6:20) are all qualities necessary for day-to-day Christian living.

Another particular principle here is applied to the workplace, and we also find it in two of Paul's letters. 'Consider what you do,' says Jehoshaphat, 'for you judge not for man but for the LORD' (19:6). Paul uses two very descriptive terms to say essentially the same thing: 'eye-service' and 'people-pleasing' are what Paul encourages the Christians in Ephesus and Colossae to avoid (Eph. 6:6; Col. 3:22). Recognizing that, whomever else we are serving, our ultimate employer is our all-seeing, all-knowing Lord is liberating and challenging at the same time. It reminds me of my school reports. We used to have two measures on our forms: 'achievement' and 'effort'. Achievement was graded by a letter from 'C' to 'A', and you would get a minus (nothing) or a plus for effort. It was always stressed by the teachers that the effort column was the most important. Likewise, our God knows what gifts he has given us, so he is neither impressed nor disappointed with our achievements. Instead he looks upon our hearts and knows exactly how hard we have tried, and how cheerful and wholehearted those efforts have been. So we don't need to worry what others may think, however wide of the mark their assessment of us is. On the other hand, it is quite sobering to think that we are included when Hebrews tells us that 'all are naked and exposed to the eyes of him to whom we must give account' (Heb. 4:13).

> Our God knows what gifts he has given us, so he is neither impressed nor disappointed with our achievements.

A valued victory (20:1–37)

We have already been told that Jehoshaphat has a courageous heart (17:6), but even he is afraid when he receives news of 'A great multitude' advancing for battle (20:1). Years before, David had written, 'When I am afraid, I put my trust in you' (Ps. 56:3), and his great-great-grandson shows the same resolve here. The phrase 'set his face to seek the LORD' conveys a real determination. Perhaps the most moving example of this kind of resolve is when we read that the Lord Jesus 'set his face to go to Jerusalem' (Luke 9:51). He knew what that would involve, but nothing would deflect him from the cross and the salvation of his people. We need a similar one-track mind as we follow the Saviour.

The proclamation of a fast (v. 3) brings the whole of Judah together to express their dependence upon the Lord. This seeking has one aim in view: 'help' (v. 4). And they need it.

Jehoshaphat's prayer (vv. 5–12) is a wonderful example of marshalling all the reasons why Judah might expect help. 'Lord, you can do it, you should do it, so won't you please do it?' There are three basic grounds for his prayer that the king presents before the Lord: what the Lord has done, what Judah is doing, and what Judah's enemies are trying to do. 'You have given us this land, we are turning to your temple, and our enemies are returning evil for good.' Perhaps the clinching plea, though, is the 'powerlessness' of God's people (v. 12). That is a potent plea to a faithful, gracious God. The power of this God 'is made perfect in weakness' (2 Cor. 12:9).

They ask for help, but through Jahaziel the Lord promises more than help—salvation (v. 17)! And salvation is the Lord's work from first to last. With language that would evoke memories of Israel's path through the Red Sea (Exod. 14:13–14), Judah is promised that they will be spectators in this particular deliverance.

Answered prayer should always lead to praise, but what is remarkable about this incident is that praise follows the *promise* of an answer. Praise precedes the actual answer, because the promise is believed. How else should we respond to the promise of a promise-keeping God, but with faith? Jehoshaphat encourages the people to believe, and faith is able to transform the most unlikely of places into a 'Valley of Blessing' (20:26; see marginal note). Then blessing leads to joy … which leads to quiet … which leads to rest (vv. 27–30).

Although Jehoshaphat got it all wrong in his dealings with Ahab (and the same weakness resurfaces at the end of his reign with another culpable alliance), we are assured that he did 'what was right in the sight of the LORD' (20:32). High places remained, but this was owing to the lukewarmness of the people rather than of their king (v. 33). Unlike his father, he 'did not turn aside' (v. 32), but kept going until he had 'finished the race' (2 Tim. 4:7).

Jehoram (21:1–20)

When Jehoshaphat's kingdom was established he set about teaching Judah the law of the Lord. Not so with Jehoram. Execution of all his brothers is the first official policy we hear about (v. 4). Another policy—his father's flawed policy of marital alliance—has repercussions for Jehoram himself and the next generation too (v. 6; 22:2–3). His father sought God (17:4), but his father's blind spot contributes to Jehoram's forsaking the Lord (21:10)—parents beware! The good news about Jehoram is that he is a leader; the bad news, that he leads Judah in the wrong direction (vv. 11–12). Revolts have no chastening effect, and not even a terrifying pronouncement of judgement from Elijah seems to make any impact. The covenant faithfulness of the Lord ensures that the house of David continues, but his justice eventually catches up with Jehoram himself. The 19th-century Scottish minister Robert Murray M'Cheyne once said, 'Live so as to be missed!'[2] Jehoram 'died in great agony' (v. 19) and 'departed with no one's regret' (v. 20).

Ahaziah (22:1–9)

Ahaziah, like Rehoboam before him, has the wrong counsellors. He stands as a reminder that if you walk in the ways of the house of Ahab, and go to war in alliance with the house of Ahab, then you're likely to share in the destruction of the house of Ahab (vv. 3–5, 7). Lot came frighteningly close to sharing in the destruction of Sodom (see Gen. 19:1–29), and there are New Testament warnings about not just *guilt* by association, but *punishment* by association as well (2 Cor. 6:16–18; Rev. 18:4–5). The only good thing to say about Ahaziah is that he had a grandfather 'who sought the LORD with all his heart' (22:9). It's an important enough quality to be worth highlighting again.

Athaliah (22:10–12)

As we read the short passage about Athaliah, it is easy to miss the fact that, for six years, the survival of the house of David seems to hang by a thread. But Princess Jehoshabeath was born 'for such a time as this' (Esth. 4:14). When God's promises appear to hang by a thread, you can be sure that the thread will hold. It held in Esther's day, when God's promises were under attack by Haman, and it held in the Saviour's day, when they were under attack from Herod. Even as the kings of Judah come and go, and the nation seems

> When God's promises appear to hang by a thread, you can be sure that the thread will hold.

to be gathering speed as it heads downhill, the Lord is still upon the throne and in control—of the nation's destiny and of the heart of a little-known princess.

For further study ▶

FOR FURTHER STUDY

1. Read Genesis 12:10–20. How did Abram get himself into a difficult situation, and how did the Lord get him out of it?

2. Read 1 Kings 1:5–6. What was David's blind spot as a father, and how did it affect Adonijah? (You could also look at the effect on Amnon and Absalom in 2 Samuel 13:1–15:12.)

3. Read 1 Corinthians 10:18–22 and 2 Corinthians 6:14–7:1. What particular kind of partnership did Paul have in mind in 2 Corinthians 6? This passage is often applied to the issue of Christians marrying unbelievers: is that a fair application? What would you say to a professing Christian who is in a relationship with an unbeliever?

4. Read Ephesians 6:5–8 and Colossians 3:22–24. How are we supposed to behave in the workplace, what is the main thing we should keep in mind, and what should encourage us?

5. Read 2 Corinthians 12:7–9. What does this passage have to teach us about unanswered prayer (or prayer when the answer is 'no')? How should it help us when we are feeling weak?

6. Read Isaiah 48:20; 52:11; 2 Corinthians 6:16–18; Revelation 18:4–5. What did Isaiah primarily have in mind when he delivered these words? What parallels did Paul see with the situation in Corinth, and why do you think the voice from heaven chose these words at this point in John's vision?

TO THINK ABOUT AND DISCUSS

1. Can you think of a time when your own foolishness got you into a difficult situation?

2. Have you ever tried to get yourself out of a fix, only to get yourself into more trouble?

3. Can you think of any apparently random events that have proved highly significant?

4. A reminder: Have you done anything yet about the 'high places' you identified in 'To think about and discuss' question 3 in Chapter 5?

5. What can the church of Christ learn about the ecumenical movement from Jehoshaphat? What criteria should we use when deciding whom to work with and whom to separate from?

7 The king with a good priest and the king who turned away

(23:1–25:28)

Jehoiada the priest earns himself a burial place among the kings, while Joash forfeits his place there through unfaithfulness. Both Joash and Amaziah show early promise, only to prove how easy it is to take a wrong turning and how difficult it is to persevere.

Jehoiada's concern for the king (23:1–11)

Joash's reign is really all about Jehoiada the priest. He is responsible for the crowning of Joash, the execution of Athaliah, the rooting out of idolatry, and a number of temple reforms as well. Even the temple repairs, in which Joash takes the initiative, are seen to be a joint venture. Yes, Joash is doing what is right, but he wouldn't be doing it if Jehoiada wasn't there. And when Jehoiada leaves the scene, Joash does what is wrong. Very wrong.

Jehoshabeath had shown great courage in hiding Joash six years earlier; now it is her husband's turn to exhibit the same courage in bringing him out of hiding. Jehoiada knows that Joash is 'the king's son' (v. 3) and he knows what the Lord has promised 'concerning the sons of David'. Jehoiada is determined to see the Lord's 'anointed'[1] on the throne where he belongs, and covenants are the way he sets about it. There is a covenant made between him and the commanders (v. 1), another between the assembly and the king (v. 3), and a third between priest, people and king (v. 16). But all Jehoiada's covenants are entered into because of his confidence in the Lord's covenant, and the promises to David it contains.

Joash is crowned in the temple to underline the fact that the one that they are anointing is *the Lord's* anointed, and not simply Jehoiada's choice as king. This is no act of treason, as Athaliah claims (v. 13); it is the restoration of the rightful king, despite her best (truly treasonous) attempts to destroy all the royal family of Judah (22:10). Then, having solemnly acknowledged that the Lord is their true king, Joash is enthroned.

Jehoiada's concern for the temple (23:4–21)

Amid the danger of orchestrating Joash's coronation, Jehoiada never fails to maintain the purity of the temple. He clearly takes his responsibility to 'keep the charge of the LORD' (v. 6) extremely seriously. He is careful to ensure that the people are restricted to the temple courts (v. 5), and that only 'the priests and ministering Levites' (v. 6) are permitted to enter the temple building itself. Even with the dramatic entrance of Athaliah he ensures that the temple is not defiled with the blood of the wicked queen (v. 14). His organization of the temple worship also carefully follows 'the Law of Moses' (v. 18), and he jealously guards the sanctity of the house of the Lord (v. 19).

Paul had a similar concern for the moral and spiritual purity of the local church. When he told the Corinthians that they must 'Purge the evil person' from among them (1 Cor. 5:13), he was encouraging the Christians there to follow Jehoiada's zealous example.

Joash's restoration of the temple (24:1–16)

Our introduction to the reign of Joash tells us that he 'did what was right in the eyes of the LORD' and it is easy to overlook what turns out to be a very important qualification: 'all the days of Jehoiada the priest' (v. 2). Joash comes across as a man of action and initiative. As he sets about restoring the temple he even tells Jehoiada to get a move on (vv. 5–6)![2] As the work proceeds we see the kingdom as it should be, with king and priest working together in perfect harmony. With the reinstatement of Moses' wilderness tax (v. 9) we see something of the spirit that characterized Israel as they brought contributions for the tabernacle under Moses (Exod. 30:12–16). The rejoicing that accompanies the giving (v. 10) must have reminded many of the time when the people had 'given willingly … with a whole heart' for the temple in David's day (1 Chr. 29:9). The re-establishing of the regular burnt offerings (v. 14) is symbolic of the renewal that the whole of the temple worship has undergone. Jehoiada has done much 'good in Israel', and always with the glory of God and the worship of God as his chief concerns. He is rightly honoured with a burial among the kings (v. 16). Doing good is often underrated.

Joash's guilt (24:17–27)

Now we learn something else about Joash—he is easily led. Jehoiada led him in the right direction, but now the king begins to listen to those who lead him astray.

We sometimes hear about important figures who surround themselves with 'yes-men'. Always getting the answer 'yes' may be easy on the ear and may massage big egos, but it could be the wrong answer. King Ahab had arrived at the point where he wanted nice words more than he wanted right words. Now Joash makes the same mistake. The homage paid to him by the princes of Judah (v. 17) certainly seems to be a factor. Joash appears to be falling into the flatterers' net (Prov. 29:5) as he starts to listen. Whom you listen to really matters. If you start listening to the wrong people, it doesn't take long before you stop listening to the right people. We have already seen Rehoboam and Ahaziah listen to the wrong people, with tragic consequences. As Joash follows suit, instead of strengthening the house of the Lord he abandons it. And abandoning the Lord's house amounts to forsaking the Lord himself (v. 20).

We have also seen Asa and Ahab responding angrily to the Lord's prophets, and Joash does no better here. God's prophets want God's people to prosper, but that means confrontation if they choose a path leading away from blessing towards judgement. David had said as much to Solomon years before (1 Chr. 22:13). When God's Word reproves or corrects us, we need 'ears to hear' or we too will fail to heed his gracious warnings. In some ways it is dangerously easy for us not to hear God's Word, because we can just keep our Bibles shut. Shutting up prophets was a more difficult task, and usually involved imprisonment or, as here, straightforward murder (vv. 21–22). What made it worse for Joash was that the troublesome prophet happened to be Jehoiada's son, but even that failed to stop the king from having Zechariah stoned. His dying words were a fitting cry for justice that was duly 'executed' by the Syrians, but the parallels with the stoning of Stephen (Acts 7:54–60) mean that we can paraphrase Hebrews and say that the lips of Stephen speak better things than the lips of Zechariah (see Heb. 12:24). 'Mercy triumphs over judgement' (James 2:13).

> Abandoning the Lord's house amounts to forsaking the Lord himself.

When you are no longer on the side of the prophets, you are on the wrong side, and even a few men will prove to be more than a match for your 'very great army' (24:24). The Lord had sent prophets 'to bring them back … but they would not pay attention' (v. 19), even though there were 'many oracles against' them (v. 27). So Joash doesn't belong in the tombs of the kings; Jehoiada does.

Amaziah's early promise (25:1–13)

The introduction to the account of Amaziah's reign

forewarns us that, while we are going to see some good things during his rule, it doesn't follow that they come from a good heart. It is encouraging that he heeds 'the Book of Moses' and shows a measure of mercy to the families of his servants that would not normally have been expected (v. 4). However, he doesn't seem to have learned the lesson from his father's reign that numbers aren't the deciding factor in battle (v. 24). Despite what Napoleon is supposed to have said, God is not necessarily on the side of the biggest artillery. Having the Lord on your side, rather than against you, changes the equation dramatically.

Numbers don't tell the whole story when it comes to finances, either. Amaziah is counting the cost of discharging his hired 100,000, instead of counting the cost of disobedience.

When we are tempted to count our pennies in an unbelieving frame of mind we too need to hear the words of the man of God: 'The LORD is able' (v. 9). The Lord spoke through the prophet Malachi in days not far removed from those when Chronicles was written, inviting the people of God to 'put [him] to the test … if I will not … pour down for you a blessing until there is no more need' if they would only give God his due from their harvest (Mal. 3:10). The apostle Paul was able to give the same reassurance to the Corinthians as he encouraged them to give

> When we are tempted to count our pennies in an unbelieving frame of mind we too need to hear the words of the man of God: 'The LORD is able'.

cheerfully: 'God is able to make all grace abound to you, so that having all sufficiency in all things at all times, you may abound in every good work' (2 Cor. 9:8). He gave the same encouragement to the generous Philippians: 'my God will supply every need of yours according to his riches in glory in Christ Jesus' (Phil. 4:19). God is no man's debtor. Do the right thing, and you can trust him with the consequences. You will never be the loser for responding positively to the Word of the Lord. Peter had his doubts and asked a question reminiscent of Amaziah's in verse 9: 'we have left everything and followed you. What then will we have?' (Matt. 19:27). The Lord's answer goes beyond 'I am able' to 'I will'. He will ensure that the right choice will be rewarded. Amaziah's reward came quickly, in the form of 'much spoil' (v. 13); we may need to be more patient. 'Therefore do not throw away your confidence, which has a great reward' (Heb. 10:35).

Amaziah turns away (25:14–16)

We aren't given any explanation for Amaziah's attachment to the gods of the men of Seir. Perhaps the only real clue is back in that short phrase 'not with a whole heart' (v. 2). G. K. Chesterton once said, 'It is often supposed that when people stop believing in God, they believe in nothing. Alas, it is worse than that. When they stop believing in God, they believe in anything.'[3] Something like that seems to happen to Amaziah after his victory over the Edomites. If your heart isn't in it, when it comes to religion, the strangest of things can draw your heart away. Paul warns the Thessalonians that to those who have 'refused to love the truth … God sends … a strong delusion, so that they may believe what is false' (2 Thes.

2:10–11). That seems to be the only adequate explanation for Amaziah's extraordinary embracing of the gods who have just so singularly failed to deliver the Edomites from Amaziah himself.

The Lord sends him a prophet to challenge him about what he has done (v. 15). Amaziah's has been the wrong kind of seeking (v. 15). We're getting used to angry responses to prophets from kings when their hearts are in a bad state, and this episode is no exception (v. 16). Amaziah probably doesn't realize it, but this is the great turning point of his reign, and of his life. That's the problem with turning points: often you can identify them only after they've happened. And when it is a turning away, it is very difficult to turn back around. Amaziah never did.

Amaziah's downfall (25:17–28)

Destruction is on its way because the king has not listened to the prophet's counsel, and it comes through taking counsel elsewhere (v. 17). Like Saul before him, rejecting the word of the Lord leads to Amaziah seeking counsel in the wrong place instead. He gets the wrong counsel in the wrong place and listens. As a result, he picks a fight with the king of Israel. He then gets the right counsel from an unlikely place and doesn't listen. What is the explanation for his unwise listening and his unwise failure to listen? '[I]t was of God' (v. 20). Defeat, capture and, worst of all, the plundering of the temple follow. But Amaziah's end comes about through a conspiracy. There is an element of poetic justice here. He listens to the wrong counsel; now others 'take counsel' against him.

Amaziah reminds us that the only safe way to do what is

right in the eyes of the Lord is 'with a whole heart'. A divided heart will pull you in opposite directions, and the wrong direction may win the tug of war. It did with Amaziah.

Teach me your way, O LORD,
    that I may walk in your truth;
    unite my heart to fear your name.

               (Ps. 86:11)

For further study ▶

FOR FURTHER STUDY

1. Read 1 Timothy 1:18–19; 5:21; 6:13–14; 2 Timothy 4:1–2. What tips can you pick up from Paul about keeping a charge faithfully (like the Levites in 2 Chr. 23:6)?

2. Read Ephesians 5:26. What is the difference between cleansing and sanctifying? Is sanctification something that happens when someone becomes a Christian, a process which is part of the Christian life, neither, or both? What does 'sanctification' mean literally? (Try looking up the word in a concordance and in a Bible dictionary.)

3. Read Exodus 12:15–19; Matthew 16:11–12; Luke 12:1. What was the significance of getting rid of leaven from Israel's homes for the feast? Why leaven?

4. Read Mark 6:14–29 and Acts 7:51–60. Compare and contrast the reactions of Herod, Herodias and Stephen's hearers with one another and with Joash (in 2 Chr. 24:20–22).

5. Read Matthew 23:29–36. What do you think the Lord Jesus meant by 'filling up the measure of their fathers'? (Gen. 15:16 may help.) How was his warning in verse 36 ultimately fulfilled?

TO THINK ABOUT AND DISCUSS

1. What unhelpful voices are we in danger of listening to in today's world?

2. What things do people believe in today rather than the Lord Jesus Christ?

3. Has there been a period in your Christian life when you have kept your Bible shut? Are you able to explain why?

4. Have you ever been worried about the consequences of doing what is right, only to find that, when you did do the right thing, the outcome that you had feared never materialized?

5. What have been the biggest turning points in your life? Did any of them only become clear afterwards?

8 The proud king, the planning king and the unfaithful king

(26:1–28:27)

Uzziah was a king who was 'marvellously helped' (26:15), only to become terribly proud. He illustrates that seeking the Lord leads to prosperity, while forsaking him leads to destruction. Jotham's reign reinforces the first truth, while Ahaz demonstrates the second.

Uzziah the helped (26:1–15)

We have seen a succession of kings being influenced in different ways by different people for good or ill. Uzziah has the best of influences in his faithful adviser Zechariah, 'who instructed him in the fear of God' (v. 5). This is the kind of fear which is a mixture of respect, love and awe. We might talk about 'reverence'—it is what is involved in 'hallowing' the Lord's name. What Zechariah teaches him means that Uzziah 'set himself to seek God'. And, like David, Solomon and Asa before him, as well as Hezekiah after him, he prospers (1 Chr. 22:13; 29:23; 2 Chr. 14:7; 31:21; 32:30). 'Seek God and prosper' is the lesson that Zechariah is trying to teach Uzziah, and the lesson that Chronicles is trying to teach us. But outward instruction and good examples don't last for ever—lessons need to reach the heart.

For the time being, though, everything looks rosy. Uzziah knows the Lord's marvellous help on all fronts; victories, border expansion, fortifications, agricultural development, military growth and an armament programme all contributed to spreading fame and growing strength.

Uzziah the proud (26:16–23)

One of his predecessors warned that 'Pride goes before destruction, and a haughty spirit before a fall' (Prov. 16:18). If only Uzziah had spotted the danger. Already some of the earlier kings have warned us that a position of strength is a position of danger. The danger comes from pride. Whenever things go well, at any level, we are particularly susceptible to this sin of sins. We want to take the credit, which all too often amounts to robbing God of his glory. As we congratulate ourselves we develop an inflated opinion of who we are. We become 'puffed up', too big for our boots. A gap develops between how we see ourselves and reality—how God sees us. As the London Underground so often reminds its users, we need to 'Mind the gap!' The rich and powerful tend to think that they can do what they like—and very often they can, at least for some time. Tiger Woods, the famous golfer, explained his marital unfaithfulness by saying, 'I knew my actions were wrong, but I convinced myself that normal rules didn't apply … I thought I could get away with whatever I wanted to.'[1] But he couldn't—and neither can Uzziah, especially when it comes to the worship of the Holy One of Israel.

For a while in Joash's reign we saw king and priest working together. Now we have a king who thinks he ought to be a priest as well. Uzziah's pride has led to presumption. He knows about the priests burning incense on the altar and he thinks, 'Why shouldn't I do that? I am the king, after all. I could do that.' But Azariah and the priests tell him, 'It is not for you … but for the priests' (v. 18). The Lord had laid down very clear guidelines, but Uzziah, by this stage, clearly thinks that he is above the law, even the law of the Lord. He acts unfaithfully, or treacherously, by stepping over the line (Num. 16:39–40; 18:7). He may have been anointed as king, but he has not been consecrated as a priest.

We don't know how Uzziah might have tried to explain himself, but the simple statement 'you have done wrong' (v. 18) leaves very little wriggle-room. The priests' additional warning that it will bring him 'no honour' suggests that a desire for the honour attaching to priestly ministry is what motivated him to enter the temple. He was not only wrong to want the honour, but mistaken to think that he would share in the honour simply by performing the same task.

Hugh Latimer once preached before King Henry VIII, only to be warned later that he had offended the monarch with his plain speaking and that, when he preached again the following Sunday, he should apologize. He began his second sermon by addressing himself with these words:

Hugh Latimer, dost thou know before whom thou art this day to speak? To the high and mighty monarch, the king's most excellent majesty, who can take away thy life if thou offendest; therefore, take heed that thou speakest not a word that may displease; but then consider well, Hugh, dost thou not know from whence thou comest; upon whose message thou art sent? Even by the great and mighty God! who is all-present, and who beholdest all thy ways, and who is able to cast thy soul into hell! Therefore, take care that thou deliverest thy message faithfully.[2]

He then preached the same sermon as before, only, apparently, more energetically.

With similar courage, the priests confront their king, Uzziah, and, as they may have anticipated, the king gets angry (v. 19). The king may be angry with the priests but, far more importantly, the Lord is angry with the king. Not only is the king cast out of the temple, he also becomes an outcast from his household and, in death, from the tombs of the kings (v. 23).

Jotham the mighty (27:1–9)

The account of Jotham is short but refreshingly sweet. He gets everything right that Uzziah got right, without making the same mistake. He grows strong like his father,[3] but without growing proud. There is a simplicity about Jotham's reign. The passage highlights one negative and one positive. The negative concerns the corrupt practices of the people, with no blame attached to the king (v. 2). All of Jotham's successes spring from getting one key thing right: 'he ordered his ways before the LORD his God' (v. 6). That is the source of his strength and what keeps him from pride. What does this 'ordering' involve? The Hebrew word could equally be translated 'prepared'.[4] The word implies careful thought and planning as he plots the course of his life and reign. This kind of discipline doesn't happen by accident.

Take time to be holy, speak oft with thy Lord;
Abide in Him always, and feed on His Word.
… Take time to be holy, the world rushes on;
Spend much time in secret, with Jesus alone.

(William Dunn Longstaff, 1822–1894)

The same Hebrew word is often translated 'established' and so conveys the added element of firmness and stability about the decisions that Jotham makes. That this careful consideration takes place 'before the LORD' suggests that prayer is also involved in Jotham's deliberations. He lives his life and makes his choices with reference to the Lord, conscious that the eye of his God is upon him, and concerned to do God's will. The danger with success is the possibility of forgetting God (see Deut. 6:10–12), but if you order your ways before him, that won't happen. And how can anyone become proud when they're doing anything 'before the LORD'?

> The danger with success is the possibility of forgetting God, but if you order your ways before him, that won't happen.

Ahaz the faithless (28:1–27)

Ahaz is another king who is easy to sum up: 'he walked in the ways of the kings of Israel'. And things had got so bad in Israel that they were walking in the ways 'of the nations whom the LORD drove out before the people of Israel' (v. 3). That means idolatry, and religious practices of the worst kind. In short, 'they had forsaken the LORD, the God of their fathers' (v. 6). As a result, Ahaz is given first 'into the hand of the king of Syria' and subsequently 'into the hand of the king of Israel' (v. 5). He couldn't say he hadn't been warned. About 150 years earlier, Azariah had cautioned another king of Judah, 'if you forsake him [God], he will forsake you' (15:2). There was no 'if' when Zechariah confronted Joash: 'Because you have forsaken the LORD, he has forsaken you' (24:20).

Although Israel is God's instrument of judgement on Ahaz, Israel is still accountable for its actions. Oded, 'a prophet of the LORD' (v. 9), condemns them for their brutality and enslaving of those they capture. When the Word of the Lord condemns us, so do our own consciences, and the best response is to go on to condemn ourselves. That is what some of Israel's chiefs do here. They have a change of heart, which results in a striking change of conduct (vv. 12–15). Judah's sworn enemy is seen treating the poor and defenceless with great compassion, carrying them on animals along a road to Jericho, where they will be cared for. Does that ring any bells? The people of Israel are, for once, being good neighbours—good Samaritans, you might say. It is unusual for Chronicles to spend any time at all on the northern kingdom, but the writer clearly wants to say to his first readers, and to us, 'You go, and do likewise' (Luke 10:37).

Once you've forsaken the Lord and you're in trouble, what you need to do is to turn towards the temple and turn back to the Lord in prayer. If you won't do that, you are going to have to look elsewhere for help. You will probably end up looking pretty much anywhere for help—even Assyria. Then you will discover that you have exchanged a faithful God for an unfaithful ally. But that is only just and fair if you have been 'very unfaithful' yourself, like Ahaz (vv. 16–21). By now the nation, and not just the king, needs humbling, so the people lose land and villages to Philistine raids. Again, a low point in Judah's fortunes is marked by abuse of the temple (v. 21). To say that it was short-sighted of Ahaz to think that Assyria could be a solution would be an understatement; anyway, 'it did not help him'.

'In their distress' Asa and Judah had 'turned to the LORD' (15:4); in *his* distress Ahaz 'became yet more faithless to the LORD' (v. 22). The next place he looks for help is Damascus, this time not for military aid but for the assistance of their gods . In fact, we are told that his worship of the gods of Damascus proves to be the ruin of 'all Israel' (v. 23). With the fall of the northern kingdom to the forces of Assyria, Judah can now be referred to as 'all Israel'. It is only a matter of time before Judah suffers a similar fate. For the first time we read of 'the doors of the house of the LORD' being shut (v. 24). Ahaz, in turn, is deservedly shut out of the tombs of the kings (v. 27).

For further study ▶

FOR FURTHER STUDY

1. Read Psalm 1:1–3 and Proverbs 28:13. What, according to these verses, is the way to prosper?

2. Read Luke 10:25–37. Do you think that the Lord Jesus might have been alluding to 2 Chronicles 28:12–15? What made that account fit his purpose? What is the short answer to the man's question 'Who is my neighbour?'

3. Read Luke 18:9–14 and James 4:6–7. What characteristics of pride can you see in the Pharisee? Why do you think God opposes the proud?

4. See what characteristics of the fear of God you can find within the book of Proverbs (see especially Prov. 1:7, 29–30; 2:5; 3:7; 8:13; 9:10; 15:33; 16:6; 22:4; 23:17–18; 29:25; and bear in mind that Proverbs often uses 'parallelism', whereby the same thing is effectively stated in two slightly different ways).

TO THINK ABOUT AND DISCUSS

1. How might we demonstrate in our lives that we are 'hallowing the Lord's name' in our hearts?

2. What sort of justification for his actions do you think Uzziah might have come up with? What other excuses do we often come up with to justify doing something we know is wrong?

3. What practical steps can you take to 'prepare your ways before the Lord'?

4. How can we stop the gap developing between how we see ourselves and reality?

5. Have you ever looked in the wrong place for solutions to a problem?

9 The trusting king, the penitent king and the proud king

(29:1–33:25)

Hezekiah is a reformer—beginning at the temple and reaching the hearts of the people. His reign is characterized by 'acts of faithfulness', with just one blip. Manasseh and Amon both reinforce the basic message: pride, bad; humility, good.

Restoring the temple (29:1–36)

There is a stark contrast between Hezekiah and his predecessor. Ahaz had 'shut up the doors of the house of the LORD' (28:24), Hezekiah opens them (29:3). Ahaz was 'faithless' (28:22; 29:19), but his successor proves 'faithful' (31:20). Anyone who was waiting for Ahaz to do something right was still waiting at the end of his sixteen-year reign, but Hezekiah begins work on the temple 'in the first year of his reign, in the first month'

(29:3). Long before, Solomon had encouraged Israel, in every situation, to turn to the temple. Ahaz and the people 'turned their backs' on it (29:6). The words 'unfaithful' and 'forsaken' describe the breaking of a covenant (v. 6), and Hezekiah uses phrases from the covenant curses for disobedience in Deuteronomy (Deut. 28:25, 37, 41). So it is not just the temple that needs repairing; the covenant does too. If the reformation began in the temple, the renewal of the covenant has its beginning in Hezekiah's heart. This isn't simply outward reformation; Hezekiah's heart is in it—all of it (31:21).

Hezekiah knows that there needs to be an urgency in addressing the situation because the Lord has been provoked and his anger needs to be turned away (29:10). An American pastor tells of a time when he asked a Nigerian woman what her long African name meant. The answer was 'child who takes the anger away'. The name referred to the way in which her parents had been forbidden to marry. They had gone ahead with the marriage, only to be ostracized by both families. It was only when their baby girl was held by the grandparents that there was true reconciliation.[1] The same name could be suitably applied to the Lord Jesus. This is what the word 'propitiation' in the New Testament (Rom. 3:25; Heb. 2:17; 1 John 2:2; 4:10) is really conveying. Jesus came to turn God's anger away from us and to actually bear it himself. For that to happen in Hezekiah's day, offerings needed to be made by consecrated priests. The Holy Place had been defiled and needed to be cleansed. The utensils that Ahaz had discarded were restored to their rightful place 'before the altar' (29:19).

The sin offering has to come first, followed by the burnt offering (29:20–24). This paves the way for praise and worship (vv. 25–30). There is a willingness and joy about the offerings of the assembly that follow. When good things start happening suddenly in lots of hearts at once, God has been at work.

Restoring the Passover (30:1–27)

The house of the Lord had been restored, and now 'the service of the house of the LORD was restored' (29:35), but the celebration of the Passover also needs to be restored to seal the renewal of the covenant. That is what Joshua had done on the plains of Jericho when he renewed the covenant after crossing the Jordan (Josh. 5:10–12). This is a covenant with all Israel, so Hezekiah invites all Israel, from Beersheba to Dan (30:5).[2] It is quite an invitation. Hezekiah doesn't want them to simply come to Jerusalem; he wants them to come to 'the LORD, the God of Abraham, Isaac, and Israel' (v. 6). He strikingly uses the name Israel instead of Jacob to underline that this is a call to a kind of reunification of Israel. The northern kingdom has been made 'a desolation' (v. 7), according to the punishment for disobedience Moses warned about long before (Lev. 26:33). What Hezekiah sets before them is the Lord's promise to those who return to the Lord, just as Moses had promised (30:9; Deut. 30:2–3). The punishment has been fulfilled before their eyes, but the promise is equally sure; as sure as the character of God. He is 'gracious and merciful' (30:9), and that means that he doesn't turn from those who return to him. On the contrary, the Lord Jesus 'receives sinners' (Luke 15:2) and teaches us that his Father runs towards them to embrace them (Luke 15:20).

We know how the Lord will respond to those who return; what we don't know is how the people will respond to Hezekiah's invitation. Will they be 'stiff-necked', or will they 'yield [them]selves to the LORD' (30:8)? The picture here is one that the Lord Jesus used when he issued an invitation of his own: 'Take my yoke upon you, and learn from me, for I am gentle and lowly in heart, and you will find rest for your souls. For my yoke is easy, and my burden is light' (Matt. 11:29–30). Oxen either stubbornly resist or meekly submit to the yoke. If the people of Israel submit, they will then begin to serve (2 Chr. 30:8).

We find that there are only a few positive responses to Hezekiah's invitation. It's a scenario that forms the basis for some of Jesus' parables about *his* kingdom. His invitation is not to a Passover; He is our Passover (1 Cor. 5:7), so his invitation is 'Come to me' (Matt. 11:28). If you have ever responded to this invitation, then you have not so much an invitation as a reservation at another feast, a wedding feast: 'the marriage supper of the Lamb' (Rev. 19:9).

> The great barrier to accepting gracious invitations is our old enemy, pride.

The great barrier to accepting gracious invitations is our old enemy, pride. That proves the downfall of many in Ephraim and Manasseh, but 'some men ... humbled themselves' (2 Chr. 30:11). While it isn't the kind of reunification that Hezekiah probably hoped for, there is, at least, a God-given unity within Judah, and 'a very great assembly' gathers (v. 13). Adhering to the letter of the law as they keep the feast proves impossible, but Hezekiah knows exactly what the spirit of the law requires: 'set[ting the] heart to seek God' (v. 19). Get that right, and you can expect 'the good LORD' to pardon much, and to hear prayer (vv. 18–20).

The extension of the feast and the great joy in Jerusalem is a high point which sends the writer back to the time of Solomon for any comparison (v. 26). It was Solomon who had prayed many times at the dedication of the temple that the Lord would hear from heaven, and we are assured here that what is happening at Solomon's temple is being heard in the real, heavenly temple (v. 27).

Restoring the kingdom (31:1–21)

Now the reformation spreads out from Jerusalem, much as the early church does in the book of Acts. We have seen 'the high places' escape removal during Asa's reign (15:17), and Jehoshaphat's (20:33), but there is no surviving the radical reformation of Hezekiah (31:1). The king's personal commitment is demonstrated by his own contribution for the burnt offerings, and the people follow suit (vv. 3–7). Again, the generosity of the people is seen to be a result of the Lord's blessing (v. 8). The administration of the contributions is explained in some detail, but one word is emphasized in such a way as to leave us in little doubt what we are supposed to learn from this particular episode: 'And they *faithfully* brought in the contributions ... Eden ... and Shecaniah were *faithfully* assisting ... they were *faithful* ... he did what was ... *faithful* ... these acts of *faithfulness*' (vv. 12, 15, 18, 20;

32:1). There are some obscure names in this section, but they were 'faithful over a little' and no doubt received the Lord Jesus' commendation: 'Well done, good and faithful servant' (Matt. 25:21–23). It is not our responsibility to be successful, but to be faithful.

Restoring freedom (32:1–23)

Hezekiah's reaction to Sennacherib's invasion (v. 1) is revealing. He seems completely undaunted, and applies himself immediately to careful planning and resolute work. We might think that his confidence is based on the fortifications and armament programme, but his words of encouragement to the commanders show clearly where his confidence lies. In these words we have a wonderful glimpse of Hezekiah's faith—an unshakeable conviction that his Lord is with him, and them, to help them and to fight their battles (v. 8).

Sennacherib thinks that trusting God is madness, and he tells the people so. He knows only about self-confidence. He paints a picture of the fate he thinks the people will be facing. That is the way 'to frighten and terrify' (v. 18). Someone has described fear as 'the darkroom where we develop all our negatives', and most of us are far too good at this kind of developing. When my children have nightmares, I encourage them to have happy thoughts as they try to get back to sleep. Paul had a similar approach: 'whatever is true, whatever is honourable, whatever is just, whatever is pure, whatever is lovely, whatever is commendable, if there is any excellence, if there is anything worthy of praise, think about these things' (Phil. 4:8).

While he may have a good grasp of psychology, Sennacherib's grasp of theology is a good deal more suspect, to say the least. He thinks that Hezekiah's God is really just one more among the many gods of the nations, and he speaks accordingly. But this 'god' is not 'the work of men's hands' (v. 19): he is 'the LORD of hosts' (1 Chr. 17:7, 24), with an army of mighty angels at his disposal. To deal with Sennacherib, he needs to employ only one.

That single angel is sent in response to prayer (vv. 20–21). Another crisis is met with prayer, and another disaster is averted. David had prayed many years before, 'O LORD, let me not be put to shame, for I call upon you; let the wicked be put to shame' (Ps. 31:17), and that is how things turn out here; 'none who wait for [the LORD] shall be put to shame' (Ps. 25:3), but those who trust in the god of Sennacherib will be. His 'god' can't even protect him in his very own temple (2 Chr. 32:21). Sennacherib had boasted that he was 'favourite of the great gods',[3] but they weren't that great, and neither was he. He also boasted about the gifts he received from Hezekiah, but it wasn't long before Sennacherib was dead and Hezekiah was receiving the gifts. 'He [Hezekiah] was exalted in the sight of all nations from that time onward' (v. 23).

Restoring Hezekiah (32:24–33)

When it is the Lord who is doing the exalting, all is well. Problems start when people exalt themselves, and that is the trap that Hezekiah falls into: 'his heart was proud' (v. 25). What makes it worse is that it all happens after another example of God's grace to him in response to prayer at a time of sickness (v. 24). God's blessings ought to humble us, and when they don't we often have to learn the hard way. 'Whoever exalts himself will be humbled,' the Lord Jesus warned (Matt. 23:12), but not if we humble ourselves first. The best thing—the only thing—to do with our pride is to humble ourselves for it.

Sennacherib returns to Assyria ashamed, but Hezekiah closes his reign having 'prospered in all his works' (v. 30) and with 'very great riches and honour' (v. 27). The only blip came when 'God left him to himself, in order to test him and to know all that was in his heart' (v. 31). That should set us praying that the Lord would not leave us to ourselves. We could even use the words our Saviour taught us: 'lead us not into temptation, but deliver us from evil' (Matt. 6:13). It was an English Reformer, John Bradford, who is supposed to have commented, as he saw a criminal being led to his execution, 'There, but for the grace of God, goes John Bradford.'[4] If we are left to ourselves, it doesn't bear thinking about where we might end up. There is no test that we are not capable of failing, and the worst of things can find a lodging place in our hearts. However, if we do what is 'good and right and faithful', seeking God with all our hearts (31:20–21), our gracious God will prosper us. Those who honour God he will honour (1 Sam. 2:30), even 'at ... death' (2 Chr. 32:33).

> When it is the Lord who is doing the exalting, all is well. Problems start when people exalt themselves.

Manasseh's depravity (33:1–20)

The opening paragraph of chapter 33 describing Manasseh's

reign makes grim reading. It is a list of abominations which, if that were not bad enough, are actually provocations 'in the sight of the LORD' (v. 6). The seriousness of these sins is underlined in two particular ways. They take place in the city in which the Lord has put his name, and they defile the specific place in Jerusalem associated with the Lord's name and presence: the temple (v. 7). There are dark hints that it is only a matter of time before Judah suffers the same fate as 'the nations whom the LORD drove out' (v. 2). They have done 'more evil' (v. 9) and have forfeited the safety in the land that they could have enjoyed if only they had been obedient (v. 8). It is all spelled out in the parallel account of 2 Kings 21:10–15. God is wonderfully slow to anger, but there is a limit, and the people of Judah are accelerating towards that limit.

As we have seen, a recurring theme in 2 Chronicles is the response of the kings to God's prophets; when the Lord spoke to Manasseh and his people, they 'paid no attention' (33:10). If you don't listen to the Word of the Lord, he may well get your attention in a way that is harder to ignore. As C. S. Lewis once wrote, 'God whispers to us in our pleasures, speaks to us in our conscience, but shouts in our pains: it is His megaphone to rouse a deaf world.'[5] Sure enough, Manasseh ends up 'in distress' (v. 12). Ahaz was the worst king of Judah before Manasseh, but there was an important difference between the two of them. 'In the time of his distress' Ahaz 'became yet more faithless' (28:22), but Manasseh prayed and 'humbled himself'. He sinned greatly, but he also 'humbled himself greatly' (33:12). This wasn't the kind of temporary humbling that avoids judgement but doesn't really affect the heart or the life. Manasseh grasped that 'the LORD was God' (v. 13). This was real repentance, and he subsequently '[bore] fruit in keeping with repentance' (Matt. 3:8). He sets about putting right in Judah what he had got so horribly wrong, and he uses his influence as king to encourage his people to 'serve the LORD' (33:16). It is made clear that a similar transformation does not take place in the nation as a whole, although some inroads are made into the idolatrous practices he had earlier promoted.

Amon's guilt (33:21–25)

It is a case of 'like father, like son' regarding the evil Amon does, but not when it comes to humbling himself. Instead, he just 'incurred guilt more and more' (v. 23). That is what we are all doing, day in, day out—incurring more and more guilt. There is only one Man of whom it could be said (three times over), 'I find no guilt in him' (John 18:38; 19:4; 19:6). The wonderful thing is that this same Man has made himself a guilt offering, so that our hearts can be 'sprinkled clean from an evil conscience' (Heb. 10:22). That is how, despite our many sins, we can hope to be found 'guiltless in the day of our Lord Jesus Christ' (1 Cor. 1:8).

FOR FURTHER STUDY

1. Read Ephesians 5:21; Titus 2:5; 2:9; 3:1; Hebrews 13:17; James 4:7. What are the different relationships in which submission is called for? How might the kind of submission differ?

2. Find the verses in Acts that chart the spread of the gospel in the early church.

3. Read Matthew 12:1–8. Hezekiah had to celebrate the Passover according to the spirit of the law rather than the letter. What does this incident in Matthew tell us about the spirit of the law regarding the Sabbath? What is the most important principle behind the law?

4. Read Luke 16:1–13. This parable teaches us about faithfulness through the shrewdness of the manager. What is the difference between shrewdness and faithfulness? How can we be good stewards of money, what are the best uses of it, and what are the signs that, instead, we are serving it?

5. Read John 9:39–41 and 15:21–24. What can increase our guilt, and what can lessen it?

TO THINK ABOUT AND DISCUSS

1. It has been said that the church should always be reforming. What do you think needs reforming in today's church? How do we know what needs reforming and what changes need to be made?

2. What has the Lord done in your life in order to get your attention?

3. What little things do you need to be faithful in at the moment?

4. How would you advise a Christian who says that he or she has confessed a sin to God and has no intention of returning to that sin, but still feels guilty?

10 The tender-hearted king and four weaklings

(34:1–36:23)

John Wesley famously aspired to be *homo unius libri* (a man of one book),[1] but Josiah could claim the same title. For a while he looks like another David, but the laments at the end of his reign tell a different story. Disappointment is followed by confusion, but the book closes by making it clear that God's plans are on track to give his people 'a future and a hope' ... and a Saviour.

The great discovery (34:1–33)

The introduction to his reign in 34:1–7 puts Josiah in the company of the greatest kings of Judah. He is given the rare accolade of walking 'in the ways of David his father' (v. 2). That puts him in the company of Jehoshaphat and Hezekiah (17:3; 29:2).

The added commendation that he 'did not turn aside' is only shared with Jehoshaphat. We are told that he 'began to seek the God of David' while he was still a boy, and this seeking bears fruit four years later as he sets about cleansing Jerusalem, Judah and the cities of some of the northern tribes of all traces of idolatry.

The cleansing is said to include the temple and then the repair work is begun. This undertaking is shown to be not just Judah's, but also involves 'Manasseh and Ephraim and ... all the remnant of Israel' (v. 9). The two vital elements of faithfulness and skill combine to move the work forward until a great discovery is made: 'I have found the Book of the Law' (v. 15). The important thing is that the book is not just found, it is also read, and read to the king at that (v. 18).

The tearing of one's own clothes (v. 19) had been an expression of deep distress for well over a thousand years. The first examples we have in the Bible of such demonstrations are those of Reuben and Jacob when Joseph had been sold into slavery (Gen. 37:29, 34). Perhaps the noblest example is that of Joshua and Caleb, as the people rebelled against entering the promised land (Num. 14:6). Athaliah would definitely get the award for the least noble (2 Kings 11:14). At times, the tearing of one's clothes would be combined with the donning of sackcloth and ashes, and/or fasting, for an even more dramatic demonstration of inner anguish (see Josh. 7:6; 2 Sam. 1:11–12; 3:31; 1 Kings 21:27; 2 Kings 19:1; Esth. 4:1). There is a sad contrast to Josiah's reaction when we look at his successor's reign just a few years later. We find out about that from Jeremiah, who tells of how his scroll with the Lord's message is read to King Jehoiakim. Neither this king 'nor any of his servants ... was afraid, nor did they tear their garments' (Jer. 36:24).

As with any outward expression of what is going on within, there is always the danger of hypocrisy, when the external becomes a performance without the reality inside. The Lord called on the people of Joel's day to 'rend your hearts and not your garments' (Joel 2:13), and Caiaphas was guilty of much the same thing when questioning Jesus (Matt. 26:65). Josiah's action, however, very evidently comes from the heart. '[M]an looks on the outward appearance, but the LORD looks on the heart' (1 Sam 16:7), and when he looks at Josiah's heart he sees that it is 'tender' (2 Chr. 34:27).[2] If we want to get God's attention, this is the kind of heart we need. The Lord has made a promise to that effect: 'this is the one to whom I will look: he who is humble and contrite in spirit and trembles at my word' (Isa. 66:2).

> As with any outward expression of what is going on within, there is always the danger of hypocrisy, when the external becomes a performance without the reality inside.

Three times Deuteronomy refers to itself as 'the Book of the Law' (Deut. 29:21; 30:10; 31:26), so what Hilkiah finds is almost certainly the entire book of Deuteronomy, or a portion of it. Josiah's language in 34:21 reflects the wording of Deuteronomy chapters 28–30 in particular (28:58; 29:28; 30:10). He 'inquire[s] of the LORD ... concerning the words of the book', the implication being that he is asking if there is any way to avoid the fulfilment of those warnings. The Lord's reply, through Huldah the prophetess, is that, although the nation has passed the point of no return, another prayer from a humbled heart has been heard. The judgement is postponed.

The irony is that, while the country has never had a better king, it has probably never been in a worse position. Do you remember Joash? He was the king who 'did what was right ... all the days of Jehoiada' (24:2). After his priest's death it all went horribly wrong. This time it's the king who exercises the influence for good. The fact that Josiah '*made* all who were present in Israel serve the LORD their God' (34:33) suggests that it was no easy matter. We are told that 'All his days they did not turn away from following the LORD' (v. 33), but the implication is that no sooner had Josiah left the scene than they did turn away.

The great Passover (35:1–27)

Following in the footsteps of Asa, Jehoiada and Hezekiah, the covenant is then renewed and backed up with action. Another Passover is celebrated, and celebrated in the right way: 'as prescribed in the writing of David ... and the document of Solomon' (v. 4) and 'according to the word of the LORD by Moses' (v. 6). Josiah's commitment to the feast is seen in his contribution, by which he says, in effect, 'this one's on me'. It is even greater than Hezekiah's Passover less than a century before. We have reached another high point in the history of Judah's kings, but we are close to some very low points in the nation's history.

Is Josiah the promised successor to David that Judah

(and 'all Israel') has been waiting for? Just when we might be forgiven for thinking that this is the king Isaiah prophesied of, the one whose period of peace will have 'no end', the one we are hoping is the promised 'Prince of Peace', we find ?him picking a fight with the king of Egypt (v. 20). While Josiah had listened intently to the Book of the Law when it was read, we sometimes need to hear God's voice speaking to us in our circumstances, or through others—even through the most unlikely sources. Neco king of Egypt is certainly no prophet, and yet his claim to be executing God's will (v. 21) is confirmed by our writer as coming 'from the mouth of God'. If Josiah had again 'inquire[d] of the LORD' (34:21) all would have been well. Instead, his glorious reign ends with mourning and lamentation (35:24–25).

The great humiliation (36:1–21)

Josiah may have looked rather like the king whose throne would be established 'for ever' (1 Chr. 17:12, 14), but his son lasts only three months on the throne (36:1–2). The kingdom may technically last for another twenty years or so, but only in the form that first Egypt, then Babylon, and finally Persia are happy to tolerate.

Don't worry too much if you find the difficult names and the quick succession of kings in 36:3–14 confusing. In a way, that's the point. The kingdom is disintegrating in confusion.

Jehoahaz is deposed and carried off to Egypt, and Neco imposes tribute and a new king on Judah. The new king is Jehoahaz's brother and he is really no more than a puppet king. His strings are being pulled by Egypt's king, who underlines Eliakim's lack of status by changing his name (v. 4). Eleven years of doing evil are ended by Nebuchadnezzar, who carries Jehoiakim (as he is now called) off to Babylon (v. 6). As the kingdom's coffers are raided, so is the temple. Jehoiachin comes next: another king with no redeeming features (vv. 9–10). He lasts ten days longer than Jehoahaz before he has to surrender to Babylon. He is now at Nebuchadnezzar's beck and call, and the call eventually comes for him to head to Babylon. The 'precious vessels of the house of the LORD' (v. 10) go with him. Nebuchadnezzar then makes Zedekiah king (v. 10). His name means 'The LORD is mighty', but the kingdom has never been weaker. Did that mean that the Lord was no longer mighty? No; it meant that the Lord's might was now working *against* his people.

Zedekiah makes the same mistake as Amon, failing to 'humble himself' (v. 12), even in the face of warnings from the prophet Jeremiah. The possibility of 'turning to the LORD' is set before him, but a stiff neck and hard heart ensure that he continues heading in the opposite direction. Priests and people are no better (v. 14), 'multiplying to transgress transgression'.[3] Way back in 1 Chronicles 2:7 the same Hebrew word used here described Achan, who 'broke faith'. Judah (1 Chr. 9:1) and Saul (1 Chr. 10:13) were also guilty of the same 'breach of faith', not to mention Rehoboam (2 Chr. 12:2), Uzziah (2 Chr. 26:16), Ahaz (2 Chr. 28:19), and Manasseh (2 Chr. 33:19). The worst transgression of all is the pollution of the temple. What makes it so bad is that the Lord's compassion in sending prophets only meets with scorn and derision (vv. 15–16). There are no tender hearts this time. Again and again in Chronicles we have seen that our response to God's Word is key. Will we have a tender heart or a stiff neck? 'He who is often reproved, yet stiffens his neck, will suddenly be broken beyond healing' (Prov. 29:1).[4]

We saw what happened to Zechariah in the reign of Joash (24:20–22), and the Lord Jesus made it clear that Jerusalem had earned a reputation for mistreating prophets that badly (Matt. 23:34–37). It was a practice that would ultimately lead to the rejecting of God's Son (see the parable of the tenants, Matt. 21:33–41). Having turned their back on the pleas of the prophets, the people of Judah will have to face the king of the Chaldeans instead (2 Chr. 36:17). The Lord has shown his people compassion, but they will get very different treatment from Nebuchadnezzar. He 'had no compassion' (v. 17).

Second Chronicles began with the building of the temple, but now the contents are carted off to Babylon and the temple itself is burned (vv. 18–19). It looks as if the temple, the kingdom and the hopes of Israel are all going up in smoke. The kingdom seems to be crumbling along with the wall of Jerusalem. But God is in control. When the Lord speaks to people his word can be ignored, but when he speaks of the future his word *will be* fulfilled. Our writer says that all this happened to 'fulfil the word of the LORD by the mouth of Jeremiah' (v. 21) … precisely. Jeremiah had said seventy years, and seventy years it would be.

The great hope (36:22–23)

Thankfully, 2 Chronicles doesn't end with a burned-out temple. The sins of God's people brought God's judgement, but his covenant promises still stand. While there was 'no remedy' that could avert the captivity, it is only a matter of time, albeit a long time, before 'the sun of righteousness shall rise with healing [Hebrew is the same word for 'remedy'] in its wings' (Mal. 4:2). In the meantime, there is the more immediate hope of return from captivity and the building of a new temple. Jeremiah had not only prophesied about the captivity, he had also told of a return.

It was the Lord who 'brought up ... the king of the Chaldeans' (2 Chr. 36:17) to begin the exile, and it is the Lord who 'stir[s] up the spirit of Cyrus' (v. 22) to get the return underway, with the prospect of a new temple. What will Israel need as they go forward? They will need what Cyrus, remarkably, wishes for them: 'that the LORD [their] God [might] be with [them]' (v. 23). And Chronicles has told us how we can know the Lord to be with us: seek God! Begin to seek him, and then seek him continually. Seek his face, seek his presence, seek his help. Set yourself to seek him, set your mind and heart to seek him, set your face to seek him. Seek him with your whole desire, seek him with all your heart, seek him according to the due order. Seek him obediently and seek him prayerfully (2 Chr. 34:3; 1 Chr. 16:11; 2 Chr. 7:14; 1 Chr. 16:11; 2 Chr. 20:4; 26:5; 1 Chr. 22:19; 2 Chr. 20:3; 15:15; 22:9; 1 Chr. 15:13; 2 Chr. 17:4; 20:3–5). Seek him!

Conclusion

In 1 and 2 Chronicles we have had lessons in prayer from Jabez; lessons in praise from David; lessons in priorities from Solomon; lessons in encouragement from Asa; lessons in reliance and perseverance from Jehoshaphat; lessons in planning from Jotham; lessons in faithfulness and trust from Hezekiah; lessons in humility from Manasseh; lessons in listening and obeying from Josiah; and the most important lesson of them all from the Lord: 'if my people who are called by my name humble themselves, and pray and seek my face and turn from their wicked ways, then I will hear from heaven and will forgive their sin and heal their land' (2 Chr. 7:14).

As we say farewell to 2 Chronicles, the book closes with Cyrus voicing what I suspect is the prayer of the writer for his readers, and is my prayer for you: 'Goodbye!' or, in its lengthened form, 'God be with you!' (36:23)

FOR FURTHER STUDY

1. Read 1 Corinthians 5 and 2 Corinthians 2:5–8. Why was it important to purge the church of the person mentioned here, what did the purging consist of, and what was its aim?

2. Read 2 Corinthians 6:17–7:1. What kind of attitude is Paul encouraging here, and what kinds of defilement may he have had in mind?

3. Read Matthew 26:57–65. What in this passage suggests that Caiaphas's tearing of his clothes is not completely sincere?

4. Read Ezra 9:1–10:5. What in this passage shows that Ezra's tearing of his clothes comes from the heart? What do you think gave Shecaniah hope, and what gives us hope when we go wrong?

5. Read Matthew 21:33–43. How does this parable relate to 2 Chronicles 36:15–16? What does it tell us about the Lord Jesus? What does it tell us about the kingdom of God after the Lord's death?

TO THINK ABOUT AND DISCUSS

1. If you were having a 'spring clean' of your own life, what would you be looking to get rid of?

2. What is likely to harden your heart and what is likely to soften it?

3. What sort of expressions would you expect to hear in a prayer from a humbled heart? (You may like to quote from the psalms or other prayers in the Bible.)

4. Can you think of a time when the Lord spoke to you through your circumstances? Or through someone else's words?

Endnotes

Chapter 1

1 J. W. Van DeVenter, 'All to Jesus I Surrender', 1896.

2 John Henry Sammis, 'Trust and Obey', 1887.

Chapter 2

1 The 'abi' in Huram-abi is thought to mean 'master', so it looks very much as if Paul had Huram-abi in mind here.

2 The Hebrew of 2 Chr. 3:3 literally reads, 'And these are the foundations Solomon laid …'

3 The Greek for 'you' in 1 Cor. 3:16–17 is plural—Paul is speaking about the church at Corinth rather than individuals.

4 Emphasis in all Scripture quotations is my own.

Chapter 3

1 From 'Small Enough to sleep', in G. Curtis Jones, *1000 Illustrations for Preaching and Teaching* (Nashville, TN: Broadman, 1986), n.p.

2 Featured under 'Winston Churchill Quotes' at BrainyQuote: www. brainyquote.com/. Accessed February 2011.

3 I've come across this story in a couple of different forms. One puts C. H. Spurgeon in the role of the elder, but I am unsure about the source of this claim.

4 John Flavel, quoted in John Blanchard, *Gathered Gold* (Welwyn: Evangelical Press, 1984), p. 157.

5 Isaac Watts, 'When I Survey the Wondrous Cross', 1707.

6 From a popular prayer ascribed to Richard, Bishop of Chichester (1197–1253).

7 From John Lavender, *Why Prayers are Unanswered* (Carol Stream, IL: Tyndale House, 1980), p. 23.

Chapter 4

1 'Jacob and Esau', sermon no. 239, New Park Street Pulpit, preached on 16 January 1859; accessed from www.spurgeon. org/.

2   Although the phrases are different in the ESV, the Hebrew is the same.

Chapter 5

1   From Paul Lee Tan, 'What Is Belief?' *Encyclopedia of 15,000 Illustrations* (Dallas: Bible Communications, 1998), pp. 154–155.
2   John Yates, 'An Attitude of Gratitude'; quoted in 'The Devil's Favorite Tool', sermon illustration at www. preachingtoday.com/. Accessed March 2011.

Chapter 6

1   Somerset Maugham, Sheppey (1933); quoted at: en. wikipedia.org/wiki/Sheppey_ (play). Accessed February 2011.
2   Dr A. A. Bonar, *Memoir and Remains of Robert Murray M'Cheyne* (Edinburgh: Banner of Truth, 1987), p. 164.

Chapter 7

1   The term 'anointed' used in this way means 'the Lord's chosen one'. The term 'Messiah' is the Hebrew for 'anointed one'; 'Christ' comes from the Greek. The actual ceremony of anointing with oil was a symbolic setting apart of the king (or priest, or prophet) for his divine calling. It also symbolized the way in which God would, by the Spirit, equip him for his office.
2   To be fair, Jehoiada was getting on a bit by this time, so a combination of Joash's youthful impatience and Jehoiada's beginning to slow down is the likely reason.
3   G. K. Chesterton; quoted at www.dailychristianquote.com on 1 October 2007.

Chapter 8

1   Quote from Tiger Woods' televised press conference, broadcast by CNN, 19 February 2010.
2   Quoted in R. K. Hughes, *Acts: The Church Afire* (Westchester,

IL: Crossway, 1996), chap. 37 (n.p.).

3 The word 'mighty' in 27:6 is the same Hebrew word translated 'strong' in 26:15.

4 As in the King James Version and New King James Version.

Chapter 9

1 Gordon MacDonald, 'Child Takes Family's Anger Away', at: preachingtoday.com. Accessed March 2011.

2 In the United Kingdom we might say 'from Land's End to John O'Groats'—i.e. from the far south to the far north.

3 From Sennacherib's own account of his reign engraved on the Taylor Prism, which is on display in the British Museum, London.

4 'John Bradford', Wikipedia (en. wikipedia.org); accessed March 2011. The oldest written account of this incident that I am aware of is in Edward Bickersteth's *A Treatise on Prayer*, published in 1822.

5 C. S. Lewis, *The Problem of Pain*; quoted at: thinkexist. com. Accessed March 2011.

Chapter 10

1 John Wesley, 'Preface', in The Works of John Wesley, vol. 5 (electronic edn.; Master Christian Library; Rio, WI: AGES Software, 2000).

2 The same Hebrew word is used in the Kings account, though the ESV surprisingly translates it differently, as 'penitent', which is more of an interpretation than a translation.

3 That is how the Hebrew reads literally—it is a form of expression denoting greatness or intensity.

4 The Hebrew for the last phrase, 'broken beyond healing', is the same as in 2 Chr. 36:16, 'with no remedy'.

Opening up series

Title	Author	ISBN
Opening up 1 Chronicles	Thomson, Andrew	978–1–84625–289–1
Opening up 1 Corinthians	Prime, Derek	978–1–84625–004–0
Opening up 1 Thessalonians	Shenton, Tim	978–1–84625–031–6
Opening up 1 Timothy	Robinson, Simon J	978–1–903087–69–5
Opening up 2 & 3 John	Crosby, Terence Peter	978–1–84625–023–1
Opening up 2 Chronicles	Thomson, Andrew	978–1–84625–290–7
Opening up 2 Peter	Anderson, Clive	978–1–84625–077–4
Opening up 2 Thessalonians	McNaughton, Ian	978–1–84625–117–7
Opening up 2 Timothy	Williams, Peter	978–1–84625–065–1
Opening up Acts	Wong, John-Michael	978–1–84625–193–1
Opening up Amos	Bentley, Michael	978–1–84625–041–5
Opening up Colossians & Philemon	McNaughton, Ian	978–1–84625–016–3
Opening up Ecclesiastes	Winter, Jim	978–1–903087–86–2
Opening up Exodus	Campbell, Iain	978–1–84625–029–3
Opening up Ezekiel's visions	Jeffery, Peter	978–1–903087–66–4
Opening up Ezra	Williams, Peter	978–1–84625–022–4
Opening up Galatians	Campbell, David	978–1–84625–190–0
Opening up Genesis	Strassner, Kurt	978–1–84625–159–7
Opening up Haggai	Williams, Peter	978–1–84625–144–3
Opening up Hebrews	Hacking, Philip	978–1–84625–042–2
Opening up James	Ellsworth, Roger	978–1–84625–165–8
Opening up Joel	Bentley, Michael	978–1–84625–191–7
Opening up John's Gospel	Paterson, Andrew	978–1–84625–194–8

About Day One:

Day One's threefold commitment:

- To be faithful to the Bible, God's inerrant, infallible Word;
- To be relevant to our modern generation;
- To be excellent in our publication standards.

I continue to be thankful for the publications of Day One. They are biblical; they have sound theology; and they are relative to the issues at hand. The material is condensed and manageable while, at the same time, being complete—a challenging balance to find. We are happy in our ministry to make use of these excellent publications.

JOHN MACARTHUR, PASTOR-TEACHER, GRACE COMMUNITY CHURCH, CALIFORNIA

It is a great encouragement to see Day One making such excellent progress. Their publications are always biblical, accessible and attractively produced, with no compromise on quality. Long may their progress continue and increase!

JOHN BLANCHARD, AUTHOR, EVANGELIST AND APOLOGIST

Visit our websites for more information and to request a free catalogue of our books.

UK:
www.dayone.co.uk

North America:
www.dayonebookstore.com

.